A
Good
Appetite

JENNY CHANDLER

A Good Appetite

Eating for Planet, Body and Soul

This book is dedicated to all the ethical growers, farmers, producers and suppliers out there. Stay strong; we need you now more than ever.

Published by National Trust Books
An imprint of HarperCollins Publishers 1 London Bridge Street
London SE1 9GF www.harpercollins.co.uk

HarperCollins Publishers
Macken House, 39/40 Mayor Street Upper,
Dublin 1, D01 C9W8, Ireland

First published 2023

© National Trust Books 2023
Text © Jenny Chandler
All photography © Kirstie Young, except where indicated
Cover illustration © Ana Zaja Petrak
Home economists: Anna Shepherd and Jenny Chandler
Design by Sarah Pyke

ISBN 978-0-00-859601-9
10 9 8 7 6 5 4 3 2 1

Printed in Great Britain by Bell and Bain Ltd, Glasgow

If you would like to comment on any aspect of this book, please contact us at the above address or national.trust@harpercollins.co.uk

National Trust publications are available at National Trust shops or online at nationaltrustbooks.co.uk

This book is produced from independently certified FSC ™ paper to ensure responsible forest management.

For more information visit: harpercollins.co.uk/green

Contents

Introduction 7

The Constant Larder 11

Winter 57

Spring 87

Summer 123

Autumn 153

The Green Kitchen 177

Every Step You Take 182

Resources 184

Index 185

Acknowledgements 192

A Good Appetite

Appetite is an urge to dive in to food – food that excites our taste buds and promises to fill us up at the same time. It has nothing to do with rules and diets, with guidelines and guilt. Eating can, and should, be one of life's great pleasures, and yet what we choose to eat is about the most powerful choice we make on a daily basis – the one with the most impact on our own health and that of the world around us. So how do we create an appetite for the good stuff? A natural desire to eat well for pleasure, health and planet?

In recent decades our growing appetite for convenience foods, for the constant availability of seasonal ingredients and for limitless quantities of meat and dairy has been doing us no good at all. Obesity rates are soaring, with all their chronic health implications, and the natural world is at a crisis point; there's never been a more crucial moment to question our eating habits.

But where to begin? There are so many angles and agendas to take on board, whether you're considering waistlines or well-being, greenhouse gas emissions or dwindling wildlife, that the subject of what is best to eat can be overwhelming. What ties this book together is the recognition that everything about us and our food system is interconnected, meaning that virtually every step in the right direction is a win-win for both ourselves and the environment.

Sourcing, preparing and eating our food mindfully is both joyful and empowering; not only are we likely to be healthier if we're mindful about our food choices, with an extra spring in our step, but we can feel that we are doing our bit for the planet too. The idea of this book is to highlight some of the driving forces and reasons for change. The bite-sized information sections focusing on subjects such as soil health, meat reduction, eating more vegetables or reducing food waste are scattered among the recipes, to

dip in and out of, hopefully sparking motivation and perhaps inspiring some further research on your part. Do check out the resources on page 184 for some ideas of where to delve deeper. It's all too easy to make resolutions, and I've certainly made plenty that have fallen by the wayside: too ambitious, too much of a sense of sacrifice or, if I'm really honest, I was probably lacking the deep-down engagement, or belief, in what I had been trying to achieve in the first place. It's important to be committed but realistic too, recognising that your green journey can be incremental; it doesn't have to happen overnight.

Many of our preferences, and even cravings, for certain foods come from habits that are difficult to break. It's worth remembering that much of the ultra-processed food that we could do with weaning ourselves off is *designed* to be irresistible. So instead of banning chocolate biscuits or striking hot dogs off the menu for evermore, try the crowding-out approach instead. The more natural, sustainable, satisfying food you put on the plate, the less room there is for anything else, without any sense of sacrifice or deprivation. Gradually our tastes and habits change. Long-term changes are not just about leaving things out, but also about discovering new options that you enjoy.

A Good Appetite is divided into two main sections. I start with the larder. By no means does this section present a definitive collection of good ingredients to keep in store. Let's just say that if your shelves contain this selection, you have the basis for some fabulously flavoursome meals. While our regular fresh purchases benefit from being as local and seasonal as possible, this doesn't limit us to a 1960s-style diet. We can certainly enhance our foraged wild garlic pesto with Parmesan, or ferment our homegrown cabbage with chilli and fish sauce.

The larder chapter is also home to all the seeds: the pulses, wholegrains, oilseeds and nuts that will become the bedrock of a more plant-centric way of eating. These seeds can effectively replace the animal protein in vegan and vegetarian diets and increase the fibre that most of us are woefully lacking too. You'll find basic cooking techniques and uses for the more readily available varieties, and discover, if you are in any doubt, that a plate of pulses or grains can be extremely tasty. Once seeds become the building blocks of your cooking, you're on the road to a more sustainable, healthy and, often, more economical way of eating.

The second part of the book is divided into seasonal chapters, celebrating what's readily available and in its prime during each season. Eating with the seasons and sourcing our food locally can reconnect us with the land and our suppliers. We become more invested in how our food is being produced and how our farmers are looking after the nature that is so fundamental to our very existence: to the climate, soil health, biodiversity, and, on a micro-scale, to the numbers of bees and butterflies in our gardens, or the sound of the dawn chorus outside our bedroom windows.

Seasonal food gives us something to look forward to; it punctuates the year with treats and fond food memories. I always think of midsummer days gorging on asparagus and melted butter when the price plummets at the end of its season, or the arrival of Barbie-pink rhubarb bringing a flash of joy just when winter feels like it might never end.

The recipes in this book are designed to be flexible, with plenty of suggestions for variations according to what's available or what you have to hand. Nothing is set in stone; the warm fava hummus will be just as good on toast with some perfectly ripe tomatoes as it is with the roasted beetroot and pot barley suggested in the recipe. Your upside down plum cake will taste equally indulgent with blackberries and apples. I hope that some of these dishes will become 'head recipes', with no need to even open the book, and that with time you'll play around with them intuitively.

You will find a few meat and fish recipes, recognising that, despite their relatively high environmental 'foodprint', many of us still enjoy eating them. The emphasis is on looking for the most ethical options and buying the best that you can afford, balancing the expense by making your occasional treat stretch much further – and making sure that not a scrap is ever wasted. My family never really noticed as I gradually reduced the beef mince in the regular ragu that I batch-cook for cottage pies, lasagne and spaghetti Bolognese. As the ratio of lentils increased so did the mushrooms and Worcestershire sauce, replacing one level of savoury depth with another. Now I've dropped the meat altogether, and both my husband and daughter have announced that they prefer the veggie ragu to the meat version. Savouring food has nothing to do with whether it's low meat, no meat, vegetarian or vegan if it tastes good.

'Good appetite' translates as *bon appétit* – something our French neighbours, who are renowned for their love of food, say to each other as they dive in to a meal. 'Enjoy your meal' doesn't have quite the same romantic ring, but it's essentially what this book is all about: relishing food that is as good for you as it is for the planet.

PIMENTÓN DE LA VERA
Denominación de Origen Protegida

LAS HERMANAS
SMOKED PAPRIKA
DULCE
SWEET

COL. CAP BON

L'ESTO

FAMIL

DESD

MARTI

ORTIZ
El Vele

SARDINAS
A LA ANTIG

Gourmet
Popping
Corn

Makes 10 Portions
or 5 Large Bowls

CAPTAIN CAT'S
MôR
SEASONING

SEAFOOD SPICE

MARET

HIERBAS
MEDITERRÁNEAS

SAL de IBIZA

Cristal de la Vida
IBIZA

GINAL ITALIAN PRODUCT

Rayner's
SINCE 1

organic
apple
cider
vinegar
with
moth

raw, unfiltered
& unpasteur

500ml

L'ESTORNELL

VIRGIN OLIVE OIL
ANIC FARMING

action of organically grown
BEQUINA olives

ODUCED BY VEA®
CATALONIA, SPAIN

CONT. 500 ML

mara
SEAWEED
Dulse
ed with rich

THE
SPICE
SHOP

TURKISH
URFA FLAKES
ISOT BIBER

WWW.THESPICESHOP.CO.UK

COL OLIVAS

ORTIZ
ATÚN CLARO
EN ACEITE DE OLIVA

THE
CONSTANT
LARDER

The Mindful Shopper

How about putting a bit more time and thought into buying our food? It's a question that will spark an outcry from overstretched, harassed shoppers the world over, but if we are concerned about our communities and the environment, it's the most effective way of reshaping our food system.

Over the last few decades, global food businesses and supermarket chains have made our lives seem easier when it comes to accessing a huge variety of food; we can, quite literally, do our shopping at the press of a button, but that convenience has come at a cost. We've lost that vital connection with where and how our food is produced, but it's time to turn things around. If we want our small producers, and suppliers who focus on both social and environmental sustainability, not just to survive, but to thrive, then we have to seek them out and give them our custom.

Most of us have a constant core shopping list, which is good news when it comes to looking for some positive changes; once you've done some groundwork and made a positive swap for a particular product, you can stick with it. There may be plenty of regulars on your existing list that already tick the boxes. That's great news, but if you're not sure about a product's journey to the shop shelf, then it's time to do some research.

A Few Good Places to Start

- Support community cooperatives and independent stores that source products from ethical local producers whenever you can.

- Check out food markets as a fun, downtime exercise rather than seeing shopping purely as a chore. Local markets provide a wonderful opportunity to get to know, and value, our producers and growers. You may find some fabulous street food stalls to tempt you too. The weekly, or monthly, market could become your source of seasonal treats such as asparagus or plums, or that occasional splash-out piece of meat or fish that you look forward to.

- Find a refill shop where you can buy packaging-free dry ingredients and toiletries. Even if it's not right on your doorstep, it may be worth a monthly mission with large containers to stock up.

If you're short of time, or don't have access to any smaller shops, there are still so many options in supermarkets and online. How about:

- Choosing to buy Fairtrade staples such as coffee, tea, sugar and bananas. This ensures that workers are being properly paid and that communities are able to invest in dealing with environmental challenges: building resilience, adaptation and ways of mitigating climate change.

- Buying loose, fresh produce and choosing the most sustainable options that you can afford. This not only has impact, but also sends messages to supermarket buyers that their consumers want a greener future.

- Signing up to one of the vegetable box schemes that have popped up all over the country, giving more of us access to organically or locally grown produce.

- Seeking out farmers, specialist growers, butchers and food producers who sell online. Increasing numbers of these small businesses have comprehensive websites where you can discover the back story of your food and order direct. It sometimes pays to join forces with family or neighbours to share any delivery charges.

As consumers it's so important that we remember, if we are lucky enough to be able to make food choices, that every pound we spend has impact. There's no point in beating ourselves up over the things we don't have the time or budget to do. It's about taking every opportunity we can to make positive changes. The more we engage with our food, the more exciting and rewarding it becomes. When we make a sustainable food choice, we are not just buying an ingredient – we're buying into an entire movement.

The Permanent Store Cupboard

While a 'good appetite' undoubtedly revolves around enjoying seasonal fresh produce, the bedrock of many dishes comes from the store cupboard.

When turning to a more sustainable way of eating, the seeds, grains and pulses that have often been considered the domain of specialist health food shops, or occupied a small shelf in the supermarket, become the backbone of the kitchen. For many of us that backbone has always been potatoes, white bread, white rice or pasta. While there's no need to abandon those familiar fallbacks, this chapter is about discovering a wider diversity of wholefood pantry staples.

Oils and Fats

Whether for cooking or dressing our food, oils are essential. It's not just about making food taste wonderful; fat is vital in a balanced diet, enabling us to absorb crucial vitamins. If you're watching your weight, it is better to use natural fats sparingly rather than over-using highly processed, low-fat alternatives; these can behave unpredictably, both in the pan and in our bodies. Here are some useful natural fats to consider:

Rapeseed oil, with its nutty flavour, is perfect in dressings and for frying (it has a high smoke point).

Extra-virgin olive oil adds its magical Mediterranean touch to anything, and everything.

Toasted sesame oil, used sparingly, lends a deliciously nutty richness when added to cooked noodles, and steamed and stir-fried vegetables.

Butter is perfect for indulgent, rich baking or just relished on a slice of good bread.

Tahini is very versatile, adding richness, creamy texture and an earthy flavour to both sweet and savoury dishes. A useful ingredient if you're going dairy free.

Nut butters can be stirred into curries, dips, sauces and soups to enrich, thicken and give a great depth of flavour.

Coconut milk, cream and yogurt can lift the simplest of dishes with their distinctive, exotic flavours and creamy mouthfeel.

Salt

Salt is essential for body function as well as bringing out the natural flavours in our food. Table salt is highly refined and may contain additives, while sea salts and rock salts, with their different blends of trace minerals, can offer distinctive flavours as well as saltiness.

Umami

Umami excites the taste buds because it signals 'protein' to the brain. This deep savouriness that we sometimes associate with meat can often be the result of drying, slow-roasting and fermenting both plant and animal products. As well as reducing the amount of salt required to balance a dish, some extra umami will help if you are turning to more plant-focused cooking. Here are some stars of the show:

Anchovies, in jars or cans, can pack an extraordinary punch, transforming a salsa verde (page 139) or adding more depth to a stew.

Dried mushrooms, and porcini and shiitake in particular, deliver a spectacular boost of fresh mushroom umami. The soaking water also makes a good stock.

Nutritional yeast is particularly useful if avoiding dairy; the deactivated yeast flakes have a nutty, cheesy flavour that adds depth to many plant-based dishes.

Parmesan has an almost utopian mix of salty, sweet, sour and umami; just a little added to a salad, soup or sauce can transform a dish.

Seaweeds, such as dulse and kelp (kombu), are increasingly available as dried flakes and powders that work brilliantly as seasoning – with so much more depth than salt.

Fermented sauces, such as soy sauce or tamari and pungent fish sauce, give an instant umami hit, while fermented bean paste, miso and even British fava bean paste can give moreish depth to dressings, soups and stews.

Sun-dried tomatoes and tomato purée are almost taken for granted but give savoury deliciousness in spades.

Worcestershire sauce, containing umami anchovies and sweet-sour tamarind, is incredibly useful and capable of lifting a flat dish to new levels with no more than a splash. Vegan versions use fermented soy instead of anchovy.

Acidity
A touch of sourness is often transformative when finishing a dish. While lemons and limes are usually the go-to essentials, other sources of acidity can give different dimensions to a dish.

Vinegars are good at bringing a whole host of flavours along with their sour kick. Cider vinegar, sherry vinegar and rice vinegar are a good trio to start with.

Tamarind is available as a paste, or a more economical block, and is a source of complex caramel sweet and sourness that works wonders in spicy dishes, rich meats and even vanilla ice cream.

Pomegranate molasses, with its deeply fruity sourness, makes a great addition to both sweet and savoury dishes. Try drizzling it on roasted vegetables.

Tomatoes in every form – canned, passata, purée, sun-dried – are ubiquitous for a reason. They are perfect ingredients to impart acidity, sweetness and umami body to a dish and always a better option than out-of-season fresh tomatoes.

Dry sour powders such as amchur (from mango), anardana (from pomegranate seeds) and sumac (from sumac berries) can all add some wonderful sour tang.

Other Big Hitters
Some larder ingredients have a blend of tastes that can kick-start the palate and breathe intense energy into even the plainest of dishes.

Kimchi and sauerkraut (see page 48) add a sourness, saltiness and umami depth that can totally transform a bowl of rice or an omelette (kimchi can be spicy too).

Olives and capers make deliciously assertive additions to Mediterranean-style dishes.

Mustard's tangy heat balances richer, fatty flavours beautifully. Dijon mustard is also a traditional emulsifier in vinaigrettes and mayonnaise, while grainy mustards add interesting texture.

Dried Herbs and Spices

Herbs and spices are miraculous ingredients, with aromatic blends capable of transporting a basic recipe across continents, conjuring up their own distinct style with nothing more than a sprinkle. Although it seems common practice for people to store them for years, the flavours and nuances will begin to diminish after about 12 months.

Black pepper has long been precious for adding its pungency to our food. Best ground in a mill, as ready-ground pepper loses its punch after about 4 months.

Herbs and spices are often cheaper to buy in larger bags, so how about sharing them among a few friends or family if you don't use them quickly enough? It's worth remembering that whole spices will keep better than ground ones, and can be toasted in a dry frying pan to amplify and enhance their flavour before grinding.

Cardamom, coriander and **cumin seeds**, plus **quills of cinnamon**, along with **dried ginger** and **turmeric** powders would be a good place to start.

Smoked sweet paprika, hot chilli flakes and a more rounded **Urfa** or **Pul Biber chilli** offer a good range of heat.

Blends are often a good way to buy spices, rather than stocking up on dozens of individual jars. Moroccan **ras el hanout**, Middle Eastern **za'atar**, a good **curry powder** and some **garam masala** are all very versatile.

Some dried herbs, such as **rosemary, thyme, oregano** and **bay**, are good to keep on the shelf, while more delicate leaves such as basil, parsley, tarragon and dill are much more fragrant when fresh or frozen.

Sweet Things

Try replacing the ubiquitous white sugar in recipes with less-refined **muscovado** sugar, which still contains the molasses, giving it character and flavour as well as sweetness. Light muscovado has a warm caramel flavour while dark muscovado tastes more treacly.

Honey and **maple syrup** offer so much more than sweetness in baking, dressings and toppings.

Dried fruits are particularly welcome in winter months and can be plumped up with alcohol for a simple pudding with a blob of custard or cream – try soaking raisins in sweet sherry, prunes in dark rum or apricots in brandy and leave overnight (also splendid with porridge). Soaking in tea is a good non-alcoholic option.

Bitter cocoa and **good cooking chocolate** are indispensable for quick desserts.

Extracts (rather than synthetic essences) of vanilla and almond are worth the extra expense.

Flour

Once a cereal seed has been ground into flour it has lost its protective coating and will begin to go stale much more quickly. White flour will keep in an airtight container for about a year while wholemeal flour will turn rancid after just 6 months, so it's worth keeping a small selection and varying when you buy. Pulse flours such as gram (chickpea), pea or fava bean flour have a similar shelf life to wholemeal.

There's no need to buy self-raising flours – 1 teaspoon baking powder sifted with 100g (3½oz) plain flour will give you perfect results.

Try swapping small proportions of white flour with wholemeal in your favourite recipes, in order to add vital fibre and other nutrients.

Eggs

Taste a really good egg from the local farmer's market and you'll remember that all eggs are not equal. It's worth researching your own regular source of eggs; some labelling can be misleading, such as the term 'free-range', which can cover a huge variety of settings. 'Organic' is the only egg standard that meets most consumers' expectations of 'free-range'. It's about doing some due diligence and weighing up welfare, antibiotic use, feed and flavour and deciding what you can, or are prepared, to pay.

As for the eternal 'in or out of the fridge' question? That's up to you, but a constant storage temperature will keep your eggs fresher for longer.

When compared with plant foods, eggs have a high carbon footprint – but they are a super-versatile, highly nutritious ingredient loaded with quality protein. The important thing is to source them well and never to let them go to waste.

If you are going away, make that last meal an omelette, using up any old vegetables from the fridge. Alternatively beat the eggs together and freeze, ready for a quick supper upon your return.

As well as enjoying eggs as a main ingredient, you can use them regularly in baking to bind mixtures together.

A Few General Larder Tips

Make sure your shelves are out of direct sunlight – jars can get hot very quickly, leading to their contents spoiling faster.

Remember that you're not stockpiling for Armageddon; even dry goods and preserves eventually go off. How about using up all the odds and ends you can find, every few months? You'll cut down on waste and save money too.

Try to have a thorough stock check every few months, so that the novelty jar of fancy preserved fruit that you brought back from your holiday doesn't languish in the depths of the cupboard for the next decade.

Limit how many open jars of jam or chutney you have on the go at once. Keeping open jars in the fridge will extend their lifespan but an entire shelf crammed with open pots can be overwhelming and often leads to waste.

Use almost empty jars of honey, mustard or chutney to make a dressing. Add the remaining ingredients and shake in the jar to make the most of the last spoonful.

Add hot water to the last trace of jam in a jar, shake and use as a cordial with iced water.

Label refill containers with the date and even the contents – grains and seeds can look very similar.

Seeds of Sustainability

When we think of seeds in a culinary sense we tend to focus on sunflower, pumpkin, flax- or poppy seeds. Chia seeds, amaranth and quinoa have been enjoying the limelight too over the last few years. It's so easy to forget that all the nuts, whole grains, beans, chickpeas, lentils and peas are seeds too. It's quite extraordinary to think that all those bags stacked on the shop shelf are just packed with dormant life waiting to burst into new plants. When you consider this, it's really not surprising that seeds are so good for us. Not only do you have the plant embryo itself, but its very own food reserve packed with nutrients to sustain new growth and, encasing that seed, a protective coat – the skin or bran – that is loaded with precious fibre.

Seeds, and particularly cereals and pulses, can form the backbone of your cooking: they are nutritious (and a very valuable source of plant protein), can be produced sustainably, store well, and are very versatile, easy to prepare, economical and delicious. Whatever your eating habits, whether you're plant based, vegetarian, flexitarian, resolute carnivore (and the rest) or you just eat, adding more whole seeds into your diet has to be a good thing.

Shopping For Grains, Pulses, Nuts and Seeds

The wonder of dried seeds is that they can sit conveniently on your shelf, patiently awaiting their moment to accompany seasonal vegetables and other more perishable food. Remember, however, that they don't last forever – particularly nuts that are loaded with oils, which can turn bitter and rancid if left around for too long.

There's no need to have a stash of every known seed in your cupboard (or larder, if you're very lucky) at any one time. You could try five of each: whole grains, pulses, nuts and small seeds, changing the variety each time you shop. This way you won't be likely to rediscover last decade's buckwheat in the shady depths at the back of the shelf. Stockpiling isn't necessary unless, perhaps, you live in the Outer Hebrides. Even the pandemic lockdowns of the last few years have shown us that, while we may not be able to get our favourite brand of pasta (or loo paper), we can be resourceful about how we buy our food. Massively overbuying just leads to waste.

When cooking grains and pulses it can be a good idea to batch cook, using up an entire packet or jar, and providing a welcome base of cooked food in the fridge for quick meals during the week, (or freezing for a later date). This puts an end to all the odd bags or random bits that don't fit a recipe. It also makes sense when it comes to conserving energy. Another approach is to make a shelf-sweep soup, or homemade granola that uses all the bits, every now and again.

If you live off the beaten track, there are some great companies online that will deliver fabulous ranges of seeds. This is particularly useful if trying to find more obscure or sustainably grown British pulses, grains and seeds (see Resources on page 184). How about clubbing together with neighbours or friends on an order to share the delivery cost?

As a general rule, when stored out of direct sunlight and at room temperature, for optimum flavour and nutritional value:

- Nuts are best eaten within about 3 months of opening a bag or buying loose.
- Oil seeds, such as sesame, sunflower, pumpkin and hemp are best used within 3–6 months.
- Whole grains will sit happily for around a year, and less if they are cracked.
- Pulses will stay in great condition for around 2 years.

The Whole Truth

Whole food, whole grain, wholemeal: for some of us these terms immediately conjure up a vision of hairy hippiedom or joyless eating. It's strange that highly processed food has been totally normalised, or even glamourised, while natural foods, in their original state, are often looked upon with suspicion or disdain.

Some 'processed' food is just fine; after all, cheese is processed milk, bread is processed wheat and sauerkraut is processed cabbage. Humans have been processing food to preserve it, and make it more digestible and palatable for hundreds of years. Ultra-processed foods, often known as junk food, are a different story altogether. These are foods that have involved modifying ingredients using high-tech machinery, using additives, flavourings and preservatives, and they're often loaded with sugar and salt too. Ultra-processed food is bad news, as we can see from the obesity epidemic hitting the very same countries and communities that rely on this relatively new, more convenient and usually cheaper way of eating. The 'western diet' is increasingly based on junk food; it's a diet that benefits multinational corporations on the one hand, and is appalling for public health on the other.

Junk food is produced with just one goal: profit, and that means getting you to buy more of it. Foods are often engineered to have a 'bliss point': the perfect balance of sugar, salt, monosodium glutamate and fat that makes them irresistible. We've all experienced the tubes of crisps that you just can't put down, and, yes, they do contain sugar. Worryingly we've normalised industrially produced food to the extent that many of us eat it at every meal. Much of it even masquerades as healthy food, with some breakfast bars and yogurts containing as much sugar as a bowl of ice cream.

By contrast, whole foods are exactly that: whole. It's not just about avoiding all the additives in ultra-processed food, but it's also the fact that, in many cases, we are quite literally stripping our natural food of nutrients.

Consider a grain of wheat, made up of the germ (the embryo of the grain), the endosperm (the food store to nourish the embryo) and the bran (the protective seed coat). The B vitamins, minerals, healthy fats, protein and fibre in the germ and the bran are stripped away during the milling of white flour, leaving us with only the carbohydrate and protein of the endosperm. Nowadays white flour is usually enriched with many of the very same nutrients that are removed during milling. It seems bonkers but at least it helps to reduce vitamin deficiencies. What is not replaced, however, is the fibre.

Fibre

One of the key benefits of eating whole foods is getting more fibre in our diets – something that most of us are woefully lacking. Fibre is basically the part of our food that passes through our system without being broken down or digested. Fibre initially slows down digestion, stabilising our blood sugar levels, making us feel full for longer and so less likely to snack and overeat. Further down, fibre feeds the friendly bacteria in our large intestine, also known as the gut. A diverse and thriving population of bacteria in the gut is increasingly linked to our own health, well-being and longevity. Finally, fibre keeps everything on the move, reducing constipation and accelerating the removal of toxins and excess cholesterol. In a nutshell, a high-fibre diet is associated with lower risk of type 2 diabetes, heart disease, stroke and bowel cancer.

Whole Grains

Beyond simply switching from white bread to granary, there are so many wonderful ways to get more whole grains on the table.

Whole Kernels, Berries, Groats and Rice

This is the seed in its entirety (perhaps with an outer husk removed but the bran, germ and endosperm intact). All can be cooked simply and then added to salads, soups and traybakes. Having a tub of cooked grains in the fridge is a bonus when it comes to preparing quick meals.

Wheat berries and **wholegrain freekeh** (a wheat that's harvested young and green and then roasted, with a herbaceous and often slightly smoky flavour), are delicious, as are wheat's ancient relatives: Kamut (or Khorasan wheat), which is a large, almost buttery tasting kernel; spelt, with its wonderfully nutty taste; and emmer (often marketed by its Italian name farro).

Spelt is an ancient cousin of wheat that tends to be easier on the digestion than the modern hybrids and has a wonderfully nutty flavour. British spelt comes from organic, or low-input, farms that benefit the local environment too. It's a win-win.

Rye berries have a slightly tangy flavour.

Pot barley and **oat groats**, which are both mild and almost sweet, are perfect for soaking up other flavours.

Wholegrain rice doesn't have to be brown; the Camargue red, and some black Asian varieties, are deliciously nutty in flavour. Be sure to cool cooked rice quickly before refrigerating, spreading it out on a large plate or tray to speed up the process, as harmful bacteria can grow quickly on warm rice.

Soaking wholegrain kernels before cooking will make them more digestible and plumper and reduce the cooking time. Don't worry if you've forgotten to soak them, just be aware that the grains will take longer to soften.

To cook, rinse the grains and place in a saucepan, cover with plenty of cold water and a pinch of salt and bring to the boil. Cover with a lid and simmer for 30–50 minutes until the grain is tender. Drain the cooked grains before eating warm or cold. Dressing with a little olive oil and seasoning while still warm really ups the flavour. Cooked grains will keep for 5 days in the fridge or can be frozen. Grains are always best eaten warm or at room temperature.

Polished Grains

Pearled grains, such as pearl barley and pearled spelt have been processed to remove some, if not all, of their bran coating. They will cook more quickly than the whole grain, are less chewy and work well in risotto-like dishes, but don't quite pack the same nutritional punch.

Cracked Grains

These can still be whole grain; they are simply broken into smaller pieces but do contain the germ and bran. With quicker cooking times than whole kernels, they can be handy for quick meals. Cracked grains such as freekeh, which have been roasted before cracking, or in the case of bulgur wheat, have been steamed, take even less time to cook (some require nothing more than a soak in boiling water). It's best to refer to the cooking instructions on the packet.

Rolled Grains

Rolled porridge oats, rolled rye and barley flakes are 'whole' as they still contain the entire grain but have been steamed, rolled into flakes and dried. They can also be used for muesli, granola, porridges, flapjacks and crumbles.

Roasted Beetroot, Pot Barley and Warm Fava 'Hummus'

Roasted vegetables, whole grains and hummus is a brilliantly satisfying and nutritious combination where the options are endless – according to the season, your taste or, in many cases, what's left in the fridge. Any leftover fava hummus is fabulous on toast with roasted vegetables.

SERVES 4

200g (7oz) pot barley or another whole grain, such as rye berries or oat groats
200g (7oz) split fava beans
2 tbsp extra-virgin olive oil or 30g (1oz) butter
2 bay leaves
1 garlic clove, crushed
Juice of ½–1 lemon
About 100ml (3½fl oz) extra-virgin olive oil
1 tbsp roasted cumin seeds
½ tsp Urfa or Aleppo chilli flakes or a pinch of hot chilli flakes
2 tbsp capers

A handful of fresh parsley, mint, coriander, marigold petals or nasturtium flowers, chopped
Salt
200ml (7fl oz) Greek-style yogurt or whipped cheese (page 94), to serve

Roasted beetroot and onions

3–4 beetroot (about 400g/14 oz), cut into thin wedges
2 red onions, cut into wedges
2 tbsp extra-virgin olive oil
2 tbsp pomegranate molasses
200g (7oz) beetroot or chard leaves and stalks

Ideally, soak the barley and fava beans in separate bowls of water for 2 hours, then drain and set aside.

Preheat the oven to 170°C/150°C fan/gas 5.

Rinse the barley and place in a saucepan with plenty of cold water and a good pinch of salt. Cover with a lid, bring to the boil and cook at a simmer for 30–40 minutes until the grains are tender rather than soft. Drain and stir in the olive oil or butter.

Meanwhile, put the drained fava beans and bay leaves into a small saucepan and cover by 2cm (¾ inch) of cold water, then bring to the boil, cover with a lid and simmer for 20–30 minutes until the beans have collapsed and turned mushy (you may need to add a little extra water).

Remove the bay leaves from the beans and blitz with a hand-held blender, adding the crushed garlic, a pinch of salt and enough lemon juice and olive oil to give you a tangy, rich purée. Transfer to a bowl and sprinkle over the cumin seeds, chilli flakes and capers.

While your grains and beans are cooking, roast the beetroot and onions on a large roasting tray. Tumble them around to cover in the olive oil and pomegranate molasses and season with a little salt. Roast for about 20 minutes, then stir and return to the oven for a further 10–15 minutes until the onions begin to caramelise.

Chop the beet (or chard) stalks into 1cm (½ inch) chunks and roughly slice the leaves.

Just before serving, warm the barley through, stir in the greens and cover with a lid for about 5 minutes for the leaves to wilt. Top the barley with the beetroot and onions and scatter with your chosen herbs or flowers. Serve with the warm fava hummus and yogurt alongside.

TRY THIS

- Not keen on beetroot? Swap in carrots, celeriac or cauliflower.
- You can replace the pot barley with wheat, spelt or rye berries, oat groats or wholegrain rice: all wholegrains are prepared in much the same way.
- Instead of the fava hummus serve a traditional chickpea version or use any other creamy pulse (page 40).

Homemade Granola

Making your own breakfast cereal ensures that you start the day with a host of healthy whole grains, nuts, seeds and dried fruit. Granola makes a great energy-boosting snack too, when it goes by its other name of trail mix: ideal for long walks or as an addition to a lunchbox.

The quantities aren't set in stone, so play around with the recipe; it's the perfect opportunity to clear the cupboards of any random handfuls of nuts and dried fruit left over from other recipes.

SERVES 8

75g (2¾oz) cold-pressed rapeseed oil
150g (5oz) honey (or maple syrup as a vegan option)
Finely grated zest and juice of 1 orange
200g (7oz) rolled oats (jumbo oats are best for this)
300g (10½oz) mixture of, or any of, rye, barley, spelt, wheat, quinoa flakes
100g (3½oz) pumpkin seeds or sunflower seeds
100g (3½oz) whole nuts, roughly chopped
Good pinch of salt
½ tsp ground cinnamon (do try ground ginger, ground cardamom or fennel seeds to ring the changes)
100g (3½oz) dried fruit, such as roughly chopped figs, dates, apricots or sultanas/raisins

Preheat the oven to 150°C/130°C fan/gas 2. Line 2 large baking trays with baking paper.

Warm the oil and honey together in a saucepan over a low heat, stir, and then, once off the heat, add the grated orange zest and juice.

Place the oats, flaked grains, seeds, nuts, salt and cinnamon in a large bowl and tip over the sweet oil mixture, stirring until everything is well combined.

Divide the granola mixture between the lined baking trays, spreading it out with a spoon so that it can toast evenly, then bake in the oven for 20–25 minutes, stirring and turning the trays around after 10 minutes, making sure once again that the granola is evenly roasted.

Once golden, stir in the dried fruit, leave to cool, then store in an airtight container or jar for up to a month.

TRY THIS MUESLI

Follow the ingredients for the recipe above, omitting the oil, honey and orange. Everything remains raw, except the nuts and seeds that you can roast in an oven preheated to 180°C/160°C fan/gas 4 for 10 minutes. Mix everything together and store in an airtight container for up to 2 months.

Simple Seeded Spelt Loaf

Despite the reported rise in home baking, and all those fabulous sourdough snaps across social media, we're still predominantly a nation of white bread consumers.

Here's a great wholegrain loaf loaded with valuable fibre that you can throw together in minutes – with no kneading, and just one rise in the tin. It has quite a dense crumb, which is perfect for serving with soup or toasting for breakfast.

MAKES 1 LOAF

1 tbsp rapeseed or olive oil, plus extra for greasing
500g (1lb 2oz) wholemeal spelt flour
100g (3½oz) mixed seeds, such as pumpkin, sunflower, poppy, hemp and sesame
10g (¼oz) finely ground sea salt
5g (⅛oz) instant dried yeast or 10g (¼oz) fresh yeast
400ml (14fl oz) lukewarm water

Grease a 900g/2lb loaf tin with a little oil (if in doubt about the tin size, it should hold about 1.5 litres/2½ pints water).

Pour the flour into a large bowl, add most of the seeds (reserving about 1 tbsp for the top of the loaf) and the salt and stir.

If you are using dried yeast, then sprinkle it over the flour mixture. If using fresh yeast, then mix it to a creamy paste with a few tablespoons of your measured warm water.

Now add the warm water and oil (including the creamed yeast, if using) to the flour and stir together well until no dry flour remains in the bowl. The dough will be wet and sticky, but the spelt will absorb a lot of water during baking. Using just one hand, mix and stretch the dough for 3–4 minutes until it begins to come away from the sides of the bowl and feels almost slippery.

Tip the dough into the prepared tin and sprinkle over the reserved seeds, pushing gently on the surface with a flat hand so that the seeds stick, and the dough reaches the corners of the tin. Cover the dough with a damp tea towel and leave to rise at room temperature for 1–1½ hours until it has risen to within 1cm (½ inch) of the top of the tin (this will depend on the heat in your kitchen – ideally, around 20°C/68°F).

Preheat the oven to 220°C/200°C fan/gas 7.

Bake the loaf for 40 minutes, or until browned and the base is crisp. Turn onto a wire rack to cool. This loaf is perfect as fresh bread for up to 3 days and for toast for up to 5 days.

TRY THIS
Play around with the seeds, using up what you have in store and mixing as many varieties as you can – each seed is a tiny powerhouse of different micronutrients.

Diversity in the Fields, in our Gut and on our Plates

According to the United Nations' Food and Agricultural Association, there are around 50,000 edible plants in the world. Just three of these – rice, maize and wheat – provide 60 per cent of the world's food energy intake.

When you walk into the average supermarket nowadays you are bombarded with choice, and yet underneath all the flashy packaging are largely different combinations and formulations of the same base ingredients. Wheat, maize and rice, along with sugarcane, soy, potatoes and palm oil, are high-yield crops, relatively cheap to produce, and can be readily processed into popular, convenient food.

Focusing on so few crops to feed a rising population makes us vulnerable. It's the old 'putting all your eggs in one basket' scenario; if a crop fails due to a new disease or pest, or changes in weather conditions, then the results can be catastrophic.

Vast monocultures have a negative impact on soil biology. Providing a single food source that favours some species (generally ones that cause disease) over others results in a loss of biodiversity and soil function. This tends to occur in tandem with other soil degradation, such as compaction. Insect biodiversity is hit by a double whammy of the lack of variety of habitat and the increased use of pesticides. It's a downward spiral.

We can all play our part, however small, in changing how our food is produced. Filling the shopping basket with a wider variety of basic ingredients supports a more diversified farming system – particularly if you can source those foods from local suppliers who farm with, rather than in spite of, nature.

The good news is that diversifying our diets is also a win for own health. When you consider

that each natural food is made up of a balance of nutrients, with varying quantities of different minerals and vitamins, it makes sense to cover all the bases by eating as much variety as possible.

Good Gut Health

In recent years there's been huge focus on the importance of bacteria and other micro-organisms that live in our gut, and the fact that processed western diets, with very little fibre, have led to many of us supporting a seriously depleted variety. These microbes, collectively known as the gut microbiome, are now said to be vital for a strong immune system, for good brain and heart health, for fighting obesity and improving mood, sleep and digestion.

Fibre, which we are incapable of digesting in our stomach or small intestine, passes into the lower intestine where the bacteria have a feast. The more variety of different fibre, the more varied and healthy the gut microbiome. There's no need to seek out high-fibre supplements; a diet rich in a variety of fruits, vegetables, whole grains, nuts, seeds and pulses will give those trillions of microbes plenty to work on. Try including a new grain or pulse or a different root vegetable or leaf on your shopping list each week, or sprinkling your cereal with a different nut or seed.

Nuts, Seeds and Pseudocereals

Nuts, seeds and pseudocereals are all important sources of protein for vegetarians and vegans. Nuts and oil seeds have a fairly short shelf life owing to the high level of fat, so they are best bought in manageable, small quantities.

Nuts are nutritious store-cupboard ingredients loaded with protein, healthy fats and fibre. As well as giving crunch to dishes, nuts can be blitzed into butters and creams, adding a richness, which is especially useful for dairy-free options. Roasting intensifies the flavour, but watch them very carefully as they can burn in an instant.

> Roast nuts in an oven preheated to 180°C/160°C fan/gas 4 for 5–10 minutes until they smell nutty and they change colour.

Choose between almonds, Brazil nuts, hazelnuts, macadamia nuts, pecans, pistachios, walnuts, pine kernels (which are actually seeds) and peanuts (botanically speaking, legumes).

Toasted oil seeds, such as pumpkin seeds, sunflower seeds, hemp and sesame, add texture, flavour and a great raft of nutrients – from protein, good fats, fibre and a vast variety of minerals – to meals. Keep a small jar to hand (page 28) to jazz up porridge, salads, vegetable dishes and soups.

Mucilaginous oil seeds, or chia, flaxseed (also known as linseed) and the lesser-known camelina, are all wonderful toasted and come into their own as thickeners. When mixed with liquid they can absorb up to 12 times their own volume, making them perfect for stirring into smoothies or flavoured milk to make a simple, tapioca-textured pudding (one of those 'love it or hate it' foods). Flaxseed is always best ground in a

> To replace an egg in vegan baking, mix 1 tbsp ground seeds with 3 tbsp water and leave for 20 minutes to thicken.

blender or pestle and mortar, otherwise it passes through the entire digestive system whole.

Both **quinoa** and **buckwheat** are known as pseudocereals because they behave rather like cereal grains as we cook them. They are high in fibre, making you feel full for longer, keeping your gut bacteria happy and helping to maintain regular bowel movements. They are also gluten free.

Quinoa makes a great picnic or packed lunch base mixed with salad, or served with yesterday's roasted vegetables. The seed is loaded with protein, making it particularly valuable for vegans and vegetarians, and rich in precious micronutrients too. Once solely imported from its South American homeland in the Andes, quinoa is now being grown successfully in Britain – a good example of our farmers diversifying.

Buckwheat is not related to wheat at all; it's a member of the sorrel/rhubarb family. The tiny pyramid-shaped seeds have quite a strong mineral flavour, particularly if you buy the toasted kasha (as it is known in Eastern Europe). Cook the seeds in water or stock and use in much the same way as quinoa. The flavour is more assertive and the texture softer; buckwheat works well paired with the sweetness of beetroot or butternut squash.

Buckwheat flour can be used in pancakes (page 29), and you'll find it as an ingredient in Japanese soba noodles (these usually contain wheat too, so are not gluten free).

Sprinkling Seeds

With a couple of small jars of ready-toasted seed mixes to hand, you can pep up the simplest of meals in a second, from breakfast porridge to salads, soups and bakes. As well as looking great, seeds will bring toasty flavour, texture and a whole host of nutritional benefits.

Simple Toasted Seeds

Heat a heavy frying pan for 2 minutes before adding the seeds (no oil required). Add larger seeds, such as pumpkin and sunflower seeds, to the pan first, shaking the pan to turn the seeds every few seconds. Once the seeds begin to pop and crackle, add any tiny seeds such as poppy, chia, hemp or sesame.

Now use your nose; as soon as you catch the nutty, toasty aroma, it's time to act quickly, tipping the seeds onto a plate or tray to cool.

Once cool, store the seeds in a small airtight container and use within a couple of weeks. It makes sense to toast only around 100g (3½oz) at a time, so that they don't get a chance to become stale.

Tamari Seeds

A mix that delivers savoury depth, tamari seeds are particularly useful on plant-based dishes and almost impossible not to snack on. Try these sprinkled on roasted sweet potato with a little grated citrus zest and juice and a dash of olive oil.

You'll need 1 tbsp tamari sauce for every 100g (3½oz) seeds. Once the seeds are just about ready in the hot pan (see above), sprinkle over the tamari and shake for a few seconds. The moisture will evaporate almost instantly. Tip out your seeds to cool and store as before.

Warm Spiced Seeds

Add ½ tbsp of the Moroccan spice mix ras el hanout, along with a good pinch of salt and the finely grated zest of 1 lemon, to the hot pan (see left) just before you tip out the seeds. Stir well, then tip out your seeds to cool and store as before.

Savoury Seeds

Add 2 tbsp of nutritional yeast, ½ tsp celery salt and 1 tsp of extra-virgin olive oil to the hot pan as soon as your seeds start to smell toasty. Stir for 1 minute and then tip into a bowl. This makes a great seasoning for plant-based pasta dishes in the place of Parmesan cheese.

Buckwheat Pancakes

More Scotch pancake than crêpe, these tick all the boxes when it comes to flavour and to looking after both your health and the environment.

Buckwheat is an unsung hero; it can grow on depleted land, it improves soil health and its abundant blossom attracts a fabulous diversity of pollinators and other beneficial insects such as hoverflies. The grain-like seed is gluten free, a great source of high-quality protein and contains plenty of fibre and those complex carbs that keep you feeling energised for hours.

The recipe is very versatile; you can make it vegan using plant milk and flax seeds, or use up dairy milk and an egg if that's what you have to hand. Similarly your pancakes can be savoury (using up that lone beetroot from the vegetable box or a handful of spinach) or sweetened with an apple. Some find the nutty, slightly bitter flavour of buckwheat rather intense. If this is the case for you, try a mixture of buckwheat and plain flour (see recommended proportions below).

MAKES 12–16 SMALL PANCAKES

The base mix
200g (7oz) buckwheat flour (or a mix of 50/50 buckwheat flour and plain flour)
1 tsp baking powder
250ml (9fl oz) milk (plant-based or dairy)
1 tbsp flax seeds, plus 3 tbsp water or 1 medium egg
Pinch of salt
Rapeseed oil or other vegetable oil, for frying

Flavour with any of the following:
1 large, or 2 small cooking apples + 2 tbsp caster sugar + pinch of ground cinnamon
1 medium beetroot + finely grated zest of ½ orange
A large handful of spinach + grating of nutmeg + black pepper

Place all the base ingredients in a blender or food processor.

Wash your chosen flavouring ingredient well. You want to include the skin but remove any inedible stalks or cores and roughly chop everything. Add to the blender or food processor and blitz until you have a smooth-ish batter.

Heat about 1 tbsp oil in a large frying pan and, once hot, add the batter in batches (by the tablespoon for pancakes or by the teaspoon for canapé bases). Once you see bubbles on the surface and the bottom has begun to crisp, turn the pancakes overusing a palette knife or fish slice and fry the second side. Serve while warm.

TRY THIS

- Perfect served with yogurt, poached or fresh fruit or, in the case of the savoury pancakes, with any variety of hummus and some salad greens.
- Try making miniature pancakes as a canapé base – reheat in a piping hot oven and serve warm.

Smoked Quinoa, Kale and Apple Salad

A couple of decades ago, quinoa was largely confined to health food shops and diet magazines, but it's truly mainstream nowadays. Good job too; it's a great source of plant protein, it's loaded with fibre plus a swathe of micronutrients, and it's incredibly versatile. Try to find the delicious smoked varieties or, if you can't source them, add a generous pinch of smoked sweet paprika to ordinary quinoa.

SERVES 4

200g (7oz) quinoa, well rinsed
400ml (14fl oz) water
Pinch of salt
½ red onion, finely diced
4 tbsp cider vinegar
1 crisp red apple
1 medium kohlrabi
1 celery stick, finely sliced
6 pitted dates, finely chopped
50g (1¾oz) chopped walnuts
200g (7oz) kale, whole leaves
100g (3½oz) Lancashire or Cheshire cheese, crumbled (optional)

Dressing
4 tbsp extra-virgin olive oil
1 tbsp grainy mustard
Salt and pepper

Place the quinoa in a saucepan, add the water and the salt, cover with a lid and simmer for 10–15 minutes. Once the liquid has disappeared, switch off the heat, leaving the lid on so that the quinoa can swell up in the steam.

Meanwhile, place the diced onion in a large bowl with the vinegar. Cut the apple into slices, skin and all, and stir it into the vinegar to prevent it browning. You'll need to peel the kohlrabi before cutting it into chunky slices and adding to the vinegar too, along with the celery, dates and walnuts.

Wash the greens well, then strip the leaves away from the tough stalks. Roll the leaves up like a cigar and slice the kale into fine ribbons. Squeeze the ribbons well to break down the tough texture and add to the rest of the salad.

For the dressing, in another bowl, stir the olive oil, mustard, a pinch of salt and a good grind of pepper together with a fork, then pour over the quinoa.

Once the quinoa is completely cool, transfer it to a serving bowl and stir through two-thirds of your salad mixture. Scatter over the remaining fresh ingredients and crumble over the cheese (if using).

This salad makes a perfect prepare-ahead lunchbox meal, since the robust greens can stand up to a night sitting in the dressing and the quinoa doesn't go soggy either. Switch up with other fruit and vegetables depending on what you have in the fridge.

Berry and Flaxseed Jam

Jams are typically a mix of about 50/50 sugar and fruit, which is a lot of sugar on your toast or porridge in the morning. The sugar acts not just as a sweetener but also to help set and preserve the jam.

Making traditional jam often involves cooking the fruit for a long time, losing lots of the vital nutrients and, equally importantly, its fresh taste. Using the thickening qualities of flaxseed, however, where the milled seeds swell up and absorb the natural fruit juices, gives you a fabulously zingy jam, which you can sweeten to your own personal liking.

Flaxseed (also known as linseed) benefits from being ground before use for maximum nutrient absorption: you're best doing this in small quantities with a pestle and mortar, or in a coffee grinder; once milled, the seeds have a short shelf life.

You could substitute the flaxseed with an equal quantity of chia or camelina seeds, as they will swell up and thicken the liquid too. They don't even require grinding but will give the jam a more granular texture.

MAKES 1 JAR OR BOWL

250g (9oz) berries, single variety, or a mixture of raspberries, blackberries, blackcurrants or redcurrants (frozen berries work perfectly well out of season)
2 tsp vanilla extract
1 tsp fresh lemon thyme leaves (optional)
2 tbsp (or maybe more) honey, maple syrup or light muscovado sugar
2 tbsp ground flaxseed

Warm the fruit, vanilla, lemon thyme leaves (if using) and your chosen sweetening together in a saucepan for 5 minutes, or until the berries have become soft and begun to collapse. Check the sweetness and adjust if necessary.

Stir in the flaxseed and leave to cool and thicken before tipping the jam into a jar or bowl. Hey presto, you're done! This will keep in the fridge for about 5 days (and can be frozen).

TRY THIS

- Gooseberry and elderflower works well as a flavour combination, using Elderflower Cordial (page 90) as the sweetener.
- Blackcurrant and star anise is also delicious – add 2 star anise as you warm the fruit, leave them in the jam as it cools, and then remove before serving.

SOS (Saving our Soil) and Why We Should Care

It's so easy to feel a lack of connection with our soil, particularly if you live in a flat, or a house with a postage stamp of a garden, and yet it's the beating heart of the planet; without healthy soil there would be no life on earth.

There's an incredibly complex world beneath our feet, with more micro-organisms in a teaspoon of healthy soil than there are humans on the planet. This life may feel like a parallel universe as we sit back and watch TV, tucking into a takeaway pizza, but our two worlds are inextricably linked. We rely on these microscopic organisms to capture carbon, protect us against flooding and drought, and to break down organic matter, recycling nutrients back into the soil.

Remarkably, there's more carbon stored in our soil than in the world's forests, plants and atmosphere put together, and a large proportion of this is bound up in organic compounds produced by fungi. For cooks, the word fungi sparks off thoughts of delicious risottos and sauces, but in fact, wild mushrooms are just the fruit of vast underground networks of fungi filaments, referred to as mycelium cells, below the earth's surface. Healthy mycelia are crucial to sequestering carbon and could become major players in our battle to slow global warming.

Healthy soil biology, including fungi, is essential for creating good soil structure (open, with lots of pores) by binding particles into aggregates and creating channels for earthworms. This good structure allows water to penetrate the soil. Organic matter in the soil acts as a sponge and can hold up to 20 times its weight in water. This is critical in drought resilience and flood prevention, slowing the rate at which rainfall enters our rivers. Plant roots and mycelia also play a significant role in stopping soil erosion.

Fungi, bacteria, nematodes and worms are just some of the millions of species that make up our soil. They are nature's unfaltering recyclers, breaking down and converting organic waste into nutrients to feed our plants in an eternal cycle of life.

Worryingly, much of the world's soil is in crisis, degraded and eroding, often due to modern agriculture. Intensive farming involves regular tilling that breaks down the soil structure, pesticides that kill life, both above and below ground, along with artificial fertilisers that impact soil health and lead to excessive nutrients in our water courses. Continuous monocultures of crops eventually lead to fields virtually devoid of life and nutrients, requiring yet more damaging human intervention in a never-ending downward spiral.

Sustainable Farming

The good news is that we can turn things around by the way that we farm in the future. Agroecology, or sustainable farming that works with nature, is on the increase. More and more farmers are realising the importance of rebalancing the ecosystem on their land. Regenerative farming, where the focus is not just on maintaining, but also on rebuilding soil biodiversity, is being embraced by more producers.

As consumers, we play a massive role. Our food choices matter. We can seek out local farmers, smallholders, community farms and producers who are both growing or raising food as well as nurturing their environment (see A Few Good Places to Start, page 12).

Buying organic or sustainable food, whenever possible, isn't just about reducing chemical or antibiotic residues in the food you consume; it's not just about taste or quality, either, but about supporting our farmers as custodians of the earth and ultimately of our future.

Organic, and other sustainably produced food, is generally more expensive than the competition because yields are often lower. It may take longer to produce and require more land or more physical labour. It's a question of balancing what we can afford; replacing some of our fish, meat and dairy with more economical grains and legumes is a good way to mitigate the extra expense with the added benefit that this will drastically lower our carbon footprint too.

We can also choose to consume more soil-friendly foods that require less input in the way of fertilisers and pesticides and can even benefit the ground they grow in. Crops such as hemp and buckwheat, along with the entire pulse family, are a good place to start, with the added bonus that they are wonderfully healthy additions to our own diet as well.

The Power of the Pulse

Chickpeas, lentils, peas and beans, collectively known as pulses, are essentially edible seeds of the legume family that grow in pods. We sometimes eat the entire legume pod, as in the case of runner beans or mangetout, or enjoy the sweet freshness of green peas, broad beans or edamame, but when we talk about pulses we are invariably referring to the dried varieties.

Reasons to Love Pulses

- Legumes are one of the few plants that, with the help of soil bacteria, draw nitrogen from the air, enriching the soil and reducing the need for nitrogen fertilisers.
- Pulses are loaded with the valuable fibre that keeps you feeling full, keeps your gut microbiome in great health and helps to keep you regular.
- They make a great alternative to animal protein, especially in a diet rich with whole grains.
- They are extremely economical, particularly when you batch cook them from scratch.

Buying

Canned pulses are extremely convenient and make brilliant store-cupboard standbys to add to salads, soups and stews. They also make sense if catering for smaller numbers.

The jars of predominantly Spanish chickpeas, beans and lentils are in a league of their own. The Spanish are particularly discerning customers; you could even say that pulses are to Spain what pasta is to Italy. These jars may be pricey, but their quality is outstanding.

Dried pulses are still the most economical way to buy legumes – particularly if you want to save energy by cooking them in large quantities (pressure cookers and slow cookers are particularly useful here). Keep in mind that 500g (1lb 2oz) dried pulses will usually give you about 1.5kg (3¼lb) of cooked. These will keep in the fridge in their cooking water for up to 5 days, ready to add to dishes or to make hummus-style dips; alternatively, any surplus can be frozen.

Cooking from Scratch

Soaking pulses before cooking allows them to cook through more evenly, creating a creamy interior while they still hold their shape. It also makes them easier to digest, allowing you to absorb more nutrients and reducing their windy potential. Some bean champions skip this step altogether, but the beans will take about a third longer to cook and this does seem a waste of valuable energy.

In general, the smaller the pulse, the shorter the soaking period and the quicker the cooking time. A pressure cooker is a boon for cooking pulses – particularly if you batch cook them regularly. It reduces the cooking times to about a third of those below, and cuts energy consumption.

Place the pre-soaked and drained pulses in a large saucepan, cover with about 5cm (2 inches) water, bring to the boil (see right for potentially toxic beans) then cover with a lid and simmer until cooked through, topping up with water if necessary. Your pulses are cooked once, when squashed between your thumb and forefinger, you can feel a creamy rather than grainy texture. Season with a little salt and add any flavourings.

Boiling There's no need to worry about toxins in your beans if you boil them for 10 minutes at the start of cooking. Red kidney beans contain lectins that, left to their own devices, could make you very poorly. Other beans such as cannellini, borlotti, black beans and butter beans do have lower, but still existing, levels of toxins too. Soak your beans (see left), drain, cover with water, then cook them at a rolling boil for the first 10 minutes of their cooking time and you will have inactivated the toxins. Rather than stressing over varying lectin levels in different beans, it's probably easier to get into the habit of starting with the initial boiling whenever you cook beans (this doesn't apply to chickpeas, lentils or peas).

NO SOAK
SMALL SPLIT PULSES SUCH AS RED LENTILS, SPLIT FAVA OR MUNG DAL. READY IN UNDER 30 MINUTES.

OPTIONAL SHORT SOAK (2–3 HOURS):
MUNG BEANS, ADZUKI BEANS AND BLACK-EYED PEAS. USUALLY COOK IN 30–45 MINUTES.

RECOMMENDED SHORT SOAK (2–3 HOURS):
CHANA DAL (SPLIT CHICKPEAS), SPLIT PEAS, TOOR DAL (SPLIT PIGEON PEAS). USUALLY COOK IN ABOUT 45 MINUTES.

MEDIUM SOAK (AT LEAST 4 HOURS):
ALL THE BIGGER BEANS: HARICOT BEANS, BORLOTTI BEANS, BLACK BEANS, CANNELLINI BEANS, BUTTER BEANS, PINTO BEANS. USUALLY COOK IN UNDER 1 HOUR (BUT OLDER BEANS MAY TAKE LONGER). START OFF WITH A 10-MINUTE BOIL (SEE ABOVE).

LONG SOAK (AT LEAST 8 HOURS OR OVERNIGHT):
PEAS, FAVA BEANS, CHICKPEAS, SOYA BEANS. USUALLY COOK IN 45–60 MINUTES (OLDER VARIETIES CAN TAKE LONGER).

Baked Beans

We Brits eat more baked beans than the rest of the world put together, consuming a staggering two million cans a day! There's no doubt about it: baked beans are convenient, economical and very popular. Making baked beans from scratch gives you control over the sugar and salt content (it's often high, in commercial brands) and allows you to play around with a variety of different beans and flavours.

It's worth batch cooking this recipe and storing portions in the freezer for busy times.

SERVES 4

2 tbsp olive oil
1 onion, diced
2 garlic cloves, crushed
2 x 400g (14oz) cans plum tomatoes
½ tsp light muscovado sugar
2 x 400g (14oz) cans haricot or cannellini beans or 500g (1lb 2oz) home-cooked
Salt and pepper

Heat the olive oil in a large saucepan over a medium heat and fry the onion for 10 minutes, or until it has softened and begins to colour. Add the garlic and stir. Once you're enveloped in its aroma, pour in the tomatoes before the garlic gets a chance to burn. Season with a pinch of salt, a good grind of pepper and the sugar. Simmer for 10 minutes and then, if you are looking for a smooth result, blitz the tomato sauce with a hand-held blender along with 2 tbsp of the beans until creamy. Otherwise, just add the beans to the textured tomato sauce.

Heat the beans for at least 15 minutes so that they absorb some of the tomato flavour. Serve on toast, in a baked potato, or with your sausage and mash – even on a pizza...

TRY THIS

Tex-Mex Beans – swap in black beans or pinto beans
Heat 1 tbsp olive oil in a saucepan and fry 2 tsp ground cumin with 2 tsp dried oregano for 1 minute. Stir in 2–3 tbsp chipotle chilli paste. Bubble for 1 minute, then stir into your baked beans. Serve with lime juice and grated zest and a sprinkling of coriander.

Greek Beans – swap in butter beans
Reheat your baked beans with 2 bay leaves, ½ tsp chilli flakes, a pinch of ground cinnamon, ½ tsp dried oregano, a handful of chopped parsley, 2 tbsp chopped dill and 1 tbsp red wine vinegar. Crumble over some feta to serve.

Italian Beans
Stir in some ripped basil leaves and a good pinch of chilli flakes or 2 tbsp pesto. A bit of butter gives a wonderful silky richness too.

Hummus

The word *hummus* means 'chickpeas' in Arabic, but has come to describe any creamy dip made from a pulse or, sometimes, even a root vegetable.

The combination of pulse, citrus and fat, be that tahini or extra-virgin olive oil, is very nutritious and can be served cold or even warmed through, allowing the flavours to really sing.

These purées are perfect as dips with flatbreads or vegetables, as toppings for bruschetta, or fillings for sandwiches; add extra liquid and you have a creamy sauce or dressing; blitz with some leftover vegetables and you have the perfect side dish or some nourishing baby food.

THE ORIGINAL

Hummus-bi-tahina is incredibly popular and very easy to throw together at home if you have a food processor or blender of any kind. If you're after silky-smooth hummus you will need to remove the chickpea skins: rubbing them gently in a tea towel until they shed is the easiest way.

MAKES 300ML (10FL OZ) OR 1 MEDIUM BOWL

- 250g (9oz) home-cooked chickpeas, or 400g (14oz) can chickpeas, well rinsed
- Juice of 1 lemon, plus extra if needed
- 1 garlic clove, crushed
- 4–6 tbsp tahini, well stirred
- 2 tbsp water, plus extra if needed
- 2 tbsp extra-virgin olive oil
- 1 tsp paprika or Aleppo chilli flakes
- 1 tbsp fresh chopped parsley
- Salt and black or cayenne pepper

Blend the chickpeas (reserving about 6 for the garnish), lemon juice, garlic, 4 tbsp of the tahini and the water together in a food processor or blender. Balance the hummus with salt and pepper, adding more lemon juice to freshen or more tahini to enrich, if required. Blitz again, adding a little more water until you reach the perfect texture.

Serve in a wide bowl. Stir the olive oil and paprika or Aleppo chilli flakes together, then swirl over the surface of the hummus. Sprinkle over the parsley and reserved chickpeas. Store in the fridge for up to 5 days.

Try garnishing with:
- Pomegranate seeds and fresh coriander
- Toasted pine kernels and slow-cooked, caramelised onions

Other Ways with 'Hummus'

Here we're talking about the entire world of whizzed up pulses – the only rules to bear in mind are that pulses cry out for lashings of citrus juice (helping you to absorb their precious iron), good seasoning and plenty of fat (be that tahini, extra-virgin olive oil or even peanut butter).

Try blending together any of these combinations. Suggestions are based on a 400g (14oz) drained can, or about 250g (9oz) drained home-cooked pulses and will make one medium bowl.

SIMPLE CHICKPEA

- Chickpeas
- Juice of 1 lemon
- 1–2 garlic cloves, roughly chopped
- 200ml (7fl oz) extra-virgin olive oil
- Salt and pepper

Try adding about 4 roasted carrots and 1 tsp roasted cumin seeds.

SMOKY BLACK BEAN AND PEANUT

- Black beans and juice
- Grated zest of 1 lime
- 2 garlic cloves, roughly chopped
- 1cm (½ inch) piece of fresh root ginger, peeled and roughly chopped
- 2 tbsp peanut butter
- 100ml (3½fl oz) extra-virgin olive oil
- ½ tsp Spanish hot smoked paprika or 1–2 tsp roughly chopped chipotles en adobo
- A handful of fresh coriander

Loosen with water as necessary. Perfect with tortilla crisps or piled into a baked sweet potato.

CANNELLINI AND PESTO

- Cannellini beans
- Juice of 1 lemon
- 3 tbsp fresh basil pesto
- 100ml (3½fl oz) extra-virgin olive oil
- Salt and pepper

A great bruschetta topping with roasted peppers or slices of ripe tomato.

BUTTER BEAN AND BEETROOT

- Butter beans
- Juice of 1 lemon
- 1–2 garlic cloves, roughly chopped
- 200ml (7fl oz) extra-virgin olive oil
- Salt and pepper

Spoon most of the purée into a bowl, leaving just about 3 tbsp to blend with 1 medium cooked beetroot, 2 pitted dates, a pinch of ground cinnamon and a handful of fresh dill. Season with salt, pepper and sherry vinegar or lemon juice to taste. Swirl, rather than stir, both purées together. Good with rye bread or crackers and watercress. Glorious in a ham sandwich.

TRY Cooking British pulses, such as split favas, or split peas to make a fabulous warm hummus (page 22) to serve alongside roasted vegetables, on toasted bread or as a dip.

Serve with pitta bread and any of the following: olives, capers, sun-dried tomatoes, Pink Onion Pickle (page 47) or caramelised onions with roasted cumin.

Chocolate, Chickpea and Hazelnut Spread

This may sound unlikely but tastes wonderful on toast and pancakes, and can even be used instead of butter icing on cupcakes (where its vegan credentials may be handy too).

This spread has much less sugar than conventional chocolate spreads, absolutely no palm oil and the bonus of some healthy chickpeas. There's no doubt that children who are used to the super-sweet commercial brands will take a bit of weaning off the sugar, but stick with it; our palates, likes and dislikes are mostly born out of habit.

MAKES 300ML (10FL OZ)

50g (1¾oz) hazelnuts, ideally blanched
2–3 tbsp maple syrup
2 tbsp extra-virgin olive oil
100g (3½oz) cooked and drained chickpeas or canned or jarred
2 tbsp dark cocoa powder
½–1 tsp vanilla extract
Pinch of salt
About 3–4 tbsp water

Preheat the oven to 180°C/160°C fan/gas 4.

Put the hazelnuts onto a baking tray and roast in the oven for 10–12 minutes, keeping a close eye on them until they smell deliciously nutty. Tip onto another tray or plate to cool, otherwise they may continue to roast.

If the hazelnuts still have skins, then tip them onto a tea towel, gather it up like a Dick Whittington sack and rub the nuts together to remove most of the skins. Once the nuts are cool, place them in a blender and blitz until well ground.

Now add the remaining ingredients with about half the water and whizz until it is a fairly smooth paste. You may have to stir the mixture, depending on your blender. A food processor won't give as smooth and silky a finish as a blender.

Now taste; if you have a sweet tooth (and most of us could do with re-training our palate by reducing our sugar intake), you may want to add a little more maple syrup. If it's too stiff, add a splash more water. Transfer to a large, sterilised jar (page 49) and store in the fridge for a week.

TRY THIS
- Play around with the amounts of cocoa and vanilla extract.
- Grated orange zest makes a tasty addition
- For an adult version, add a couple of prunes soaked overnight in rum.
- It's worth roasting at least a double batch of hazelnuts to utilise the oven heat. Once cool, store in a jar and use within a month. Perfect for sprinkling on salads.

Dal

Economical, sustainable, nutritious, easy to prepare and so good to eat. Bread may have been described as the 'staff of life' for much of the world, but when it comes to the Indian subcontinent, that title would surely go to dal. Although sometimes referred to as 'poor man's meat', down to its vital role in nourishing millions of impoverished people, you'll still find dal on the most lavish of Indian tables.

Served with flatbread or rice, you have a great source of protein and fibre, and if accompanied by some fresh vegetables and yogurt, you have a perfectly balanced, frugal feast. The dal itself will be mildly flavoured, but what gives its character and kick is commonly known as the tempering or tarka. This is a mixture of spices and aromatics, and possibly onions, shallots or garlic, that are fried and stirred in just before serving (see overleaf).

SERVES 4 AS A MAIN WITH FLATBREAD OR RICE, OR 8 AS A SIDE DISH

400g (14oz) red lentils (masoor dal), rinsed
1.2 litres (2 pints) water
5cm (2-inch) finger of fresh root ginger, peeled and roughly chopped
2 garlic cloves, finely chopped
1 tsp ground turmeric
½–1 tsp salt
2 tbsp fresh chopped coriander
Squeeze of lime or lemon juice

Add the lentils to a large saucepan with the water. Add the ginger, garlic and turmeric, then gently bubble away, partially covered with the lid, for about 1 hour, stirring occasionally and adding more water if the dal is getting very thick.

Once the lentils have collapsed, season with the salt and add more water if you prefer a looser consistency; traditional dal can vary from a soupy texture to that of a thick porridge, so the choice is yours. Add your tarka of choice (see page 46) and then sprinkle with the coriander and lemon juice.

(see page 46)

TRY THIS

- Replace the lentils with mung dal (split mung beans), urid dal (split black urid beans) or, with slightly longer cooking times, chana dal (split chickpeas), matar dal (split peas) or toor dal (split pigeon peas).
- Replace 400ml (14fl oz) of the water with a 400ml (14fl oz) can coconut milk for a richer dal, or with a 400g (14oz) can chopped tomatoes for something more acidic; you could even go wild and throw in both.
- Try stirring a couple of handfuls of chopped spinach into the dal just before serving.

Tarkas to Try

The tarka, or tadka or tempering, is a classic cooking technique used throughout South Asia. The frying of spices and aromatics over a high heat makes them bloom, unlocking their intense flavour and perfume, while simultaneously infusing the cooking oil or ghee.

Every region, every family and every cook will have their own favourite combinations; nothing is set in stone. Here are a few ideas to set you on your way, and then it's time to play with your own creations.

Take great care not to burn your spices; as soon as you're enveloped in their magical scent it's time to tip them over your dal before they scorch and taste bitter.

VARIATIONS
Heat 2 generous tbsp ghee, butter or vegetable oil in a small frying pan.

Continue with any of the suggestions below before stirring the hot tarka into your dal and checking the seasoning before serving the ultimate comfort food with flatbreads or rice and a fresh, crunchy pickle (opposite).

Continue with any of the following:
- 1 onion, sliced
- ½ tsp cumin seeds
- 3–4 fresh green chillies, sliced

Fry the onion until golden, then add the cumin seeds and chillies and fry for a moment or two, or until they take your breath away.

OR
- 1 tsp black mustard seeds
- 12 fresh curry leaves
- ½–1 tsp crushed chilli flakes

Fry the mustard seeds until they sputter, then add the curry leaves and chilli and cook for another 30 seconds.

OR
- 1 tsp ground coriander
- ½ tsp garam masala
- 2 tsp fenugreek seeds
- 4 small tomatoes, chopped

Add the spices to the pan and fry until you are enveloped in aromas, then immediately add the tomato to calm the pan (it's all too easy to burn ground spices). Soften the tomato for 2 minutes.

OR
- 2 cinnamon sticks
- 2 cardamom pods, crushed
- 1 bay leaf
- 1 tsp cumin seeds
- 1 onion, sliced

Fry the cinnamon, cardamom, bay leaf and cumin until you can smell the individual spices, then stir in the onion to temper the heat. Fry gently until soft.

Quick Pickles

The perfect way to inject a bit of instant ping, punch, bite and crunch to dals, soups, dips and just about anything savoury. These differ from chutneys and traditional British pickles in that they are thrown together in minutes and aren't designed to be preserved for any great length of time – this generally means a drastic reduction in sugar and salt, and a much crispier, fresher flavour.

PINK ONION PICKLE

MAKES 200ML (7FL OZ) OR 1 SMALL BOWL

- ½ tsp salt
- ½ tsp light muscovado sugar
- 2 tbsp white wine vinegar
- 1 red onion, finely sliced

This couldn't be easier. Mix the salt, sugar and vinegar together, then pour over the sliced onion in a small bowl. Turn the onion over in the liquid and within 10 minutes you'll have Barbie-pink, sweet and sour onion. Serve.

INSTANT PICKLED CUCUMBER OR COURGETTE

MAKES 200ML (7FL OZ) OR 1 SMALL BOWL

- 200g (7oz) cucumber or courgette, finely sliced
- ½ tsp salt
- ½ tsp light muscovado sugar
- 2 tbsp white wine vinegar
- 1 tsp coriander seeds, roasted and roughly crushed

Gently massage the slices of cucumber or courgette with the remaining ingredients and leave to rest and 'pickle' for 10 minutes before serving.

SPICED CARROT OR CAULIFLOWER PICKLE

MAKES 300ML (10FL OZ) OR 1 MEDIUM BOWL

- 1 tbsp vegetable oil
- 1 tsp mustard seeds
- ½ tsp fenugreek seeds
- 12 fresh curry leaves
- 1 tsp grated fresh root ginger
- 2–3 carrots, cut into matchsticks or 200g (7oz) finely sliced cauliflower florets, or a mixture of both
- 1 fresh red chilli, finely sliced (optional)
- Pinch of salt
- 1–2 tsp light muscovado sugar or jaggery
- A little finely grated zest and the juice of 1 lemon or lime
- 1 tbsp cider vinegar (optional)

Heat the oil in a frying pan, then add the mustard seeds, fenugreek seeds and curry leaves and fry until they spit and splutter. Add the ginger, your chosen vegetable(s) and the chilli, if using, stirring over the heat for just a minute or two. Remove from the heat and season with the salt, sugar, lime zest and juice, adding a dash of vinegar if you're after a bit more of a zing. Serve.

Fermented Foods for a Flourishing Flora

The buzz around fermented food is fairly recent; you could even be forgiven for thinking of it as another fad. Yet so many of our daily essentials, as well as favourite treats, are fermented: bread, tea, cheese, soy sauce, chocolate, beer and wine are among the most common examples. Humans have used fermentation for millennia to make food more palatable, digestible, exciting or quite simply to preserve it for leaner times (and it certainly is a highly sustainable and economical way to deal with a glut of vegetables).

Scientists are constantly discovering the benefits of consuming live fermented food, where the active bacteria are still present because of the lack of pasteurisation or cooking. These foods, known as probiotic foods, can boost the diversity of microbes in our lower intestine, and having a rich gut microbiome (or 'gut flora') is increasingly linked to good health, longevity and even happiness. There is a huge amount of fascinating research to delve into, both online and in print (see Resources on page 184).

I have already mentioned these bacteria on page 20 when looking at the benefits of eating more whole foods. Pulses, grains, nuts and seeds contain plenty of fibre that sustain and feed our gut bacteria. These are known as prebiotic foods while the live fermented, probiotic foods can replenish and renew the microbes themselves.

Given that probiotic products, such as kefir, kombucha, kimchi and sauerkraut are delicious (read 'virtually addictive', once you've developed a taste for them), it's a no-brainer to try and eat more of them. Eastern and central European, as well as Asian, cultures have enjoyed the complex taste and depth that so many of these fermented foods impart for thousands of years, so we have some catching up to do.

Making your own sauerkraut is perfect entry-level fermentation, so do give it a go.

SIMPLE RUBY SAUERKRAUT

You can, of course, use a white cabbage for your kraut, but red cabbage produces such an extraordinarily dramatic colour that it's got to be a winner. Serve the tangy sauerkraut with dishes such as the Bubble and Squeak on page 100, in a cheese toastie, with roasted vegetables, on top of soup – the options are infinite.

MAKES A 1-LITRE (34FL OZ) JAR

Remove the outer leaves of 1 red cabbage, quarter, and then cut away the hard core. Now finely slice the cabbage, wash and drain, then place in a large bowl set over some scales. Weigh and calculate 2g (½ tsp) sea salt for every 100g (3½oz) cabbage.

Sprinkle over the salt and massage the cabbage for about 5–10 minutes until you have a pool of brine.

Pack the cabbage down into a sterilised 1 litre/ 34fl oz Kilner jar (right) or another large jar (a jam funnel is useful here), pushing down with a wooden spoon to get rid of any air gaps and tipping over the salty brine left in the bowl.

Place a weight on top (see 'Covering with brine' opposite) and make sure that the cabbage is submerged by at least 1cm (½ inch) of liquid. Leave about 3–4cm (1¼–1½ inches) in the jar for expansion and close the lid (making sure the gas can escape, see opposite). Place the jar on a tray or plate away from direct sunlight and leave to ferment at room temperature for 2–6 weeks. Once you like the taste, store in the fridge.

Try this:
- Add about 3 tsp caraway seeds to the massaged cabbage before placing it in the jar.
- Mix the cabbage with finely sliced carrot, kohlrabi, beetroot or fennel.
- Pep up the mix with 2 tsp grated fresh root ginger, or turmeric, or both.

General Fermenting Know-how
Sterilising jars
Wash jars with hot soapy water. Don't dry them, but heat them through in an oven preheated to 160°C/140°C fan/gas 3 for 10 minutes. Lids or rubber seals need to be soaked separately in a pan of boiling water for 10 minutes.

Covering with brine
Fermenting vegetables relies on the naturally occurring lactic acid bacteria found in plants; these are anaerobic (meaning that they live and thrive without oxygen). The anaerobic bacteria feast on the natural sugars in fruit and vegetables to produce the lactic acid, giving that characteristic tangy taste. While the ingredients are submerged in brine, harmful bacteria are prevented from growing by both the salt and the lack of oxygen – always make sure that the cabbage (or chosen vegetables) are completely covered in the salty liquid at all times. You can weigh the vegetables down below the liquid surface with a specially designed glass weight, a small plastic bag filled with water (or brine, just in case it bursts), or a piece of food-safe plastic, such as a piece of plastic cut from a yogurt pot, cut to fit snugly below the shoulders of your jar.

Letting the gas out
While the lactic acid bacteria are busy gorging themselves, they will produce little bubbles of carbon dioxide, which is a good sign, but these will need to escape from the jar (otherwise there may be an unwelcome explosion!). Removing the rubber seal from around a Kilner jar and securing the metal catch with an elastic band instead of clamping it down will allow some gas to escape naturally, or airlock lids are available (which will let the carbon dioxide out of the jar while preventing oxygen from getting in). Place your jar on a tray or plate to catch any escaping liquid during the fermentation process.

How long to ferment for?
At an average room temperature of around 18–22°C/64–72°F, out of direct sunlight, your fermented vegetables will just begin to taste interestingly tangy after about 10 days. Remember to always use clean cutlery when tasting, otherwise you may introduce unwelcome bacteria into the mix. Once you're happy with the flavour you can refrigerate the jar to halt the fermentation process, but it's up to you – the ferment will taste increasingly funky and assertive the longer you leave it, until it eventually becomes unpalatable. It's all about experimentation and personal taste.

Waste Not, Want Not

When we talk about waste, the discussion focuses, more often than not, on the most sustainable ways to recycle, or dispose of, it. We've come to accept that rubbish is just a natural part of modern life – when it's actually anything *but* natural.

Waste is a human invention, whereas nature, by contrast, is an ecosystem that works in cycles; in a simplified example, plants grow in soil, animals eat plants, dung replenishes soil... no waste.

So, as the inventors of waste, we now need to turn full circle and work out, not just how to process our rubbish more effectively, but how to stop creating trash in the first place. We simply have to cut back. When it comes to clothing, toys, household gadgets and other purchases, we can be more mindful, and question whether we *need* to replace or throw something out; could we mend, upcycle or just do without the latest model? Food, on the other hand, is something that we all obviously need to buy.

Avoiding excess packaging, and particularly single-use plastics, can be quite complicated, but there are plenty of tips on how to reduce your general household waste on page 180. However, perhaps the most alarming problem of all is the waste of food itself.

Globally we are wasting around a third of the food we produce. Meanwhile, the United Nations estimates that as many as 800 million people were going hungry on a daily basis in 2020 – that's over 10 per cent of the total population. We currently produce enough food to feed the world and yet so much of it ends up in the bin; it's just immoral. Feeding the rapidly expanding population is one of mankind's greatest challenges, so cutting food waste is such an obvious place to start.

Food Waste is Driving Climate Change by Emitting Greenhouse Gases

When we waste food we also squander the energy, the resources and all the associated carbon emissions that go into its production, processing, transportation and cooking. In fact, if food waste were a country it would be the third largest producer of carbon dioxide in the world, after the USA and China. To make matters worse, a vast proportion of discarded food ends up in landfill generating methane gas. Don't forget that the last resort for uneaten food has to be the compost and never the bin.

Precious habitats are being lost to expanding farmland every day, in order to grow, or rear, our food. Surely cutting food waste, as well as reducing our appetite for meat (page 76) means that some of that land could be returned to the wild?

A proportion of produce never even makes it onto the market stall or shop shelf. Food spoilage is all too common, and particularly in the developing world where the lack of efficient storage facilities, or transportation, is a colossal problem. More innovation and investment are certainly needed for sustainable projects such as supplying solar-powered community fridges and other post-harvest technology.

Closer to home, we have a situation where food is left to rot in our fields, as supermarket buyers deem the fruit or vegetable too big, too small, too misshapen, or too plain ugly for us to want to buy. Try to snap up the 'wonky' vegetables in your local stores to show that we champion taste, sustainability and fair treatment of our farmers over appearance. Wonky food box schemes are another option and can be reasonably inexpensive.

Labour shortages are the latest hurdle for our food system, with tales of perfectly good food being left unpicked and thousands of pigs being culled due to a lack of agricultural and abattoir workers.

Retail and hospitality businesses are, quite rightly, under increasing pressure to reduce their food waste. Some pioneering producers, restaurants and cafés make their zero-waste policy a key part of their identity; they need our custom (and often serve fabulously creative dishes). We need a ripple effect whereby ethical businesses thrive and there's a financial incentive to being green.

The all-too-common sight of commercial bins behind premises, filled with perfectly edible 'out of date' (see Understanding Date Labels on page 53) products, is thankfully on the wane. Supporting charitable organisations, such as Fare Share, The Felix Project and Plan Zheroes, is crucial as they play a vital role in redistributing valuable food to community projects feeding our most vulnerable. It's a win-win, helping to provide for the growing number of people who are, quite literally, on the bread line, while reducing the environmental footprint of our food system.

Then there's the vast amount of food that we waste in our own homes. Let's look at how we can tackle it:

- Food Shopping (right)
- Optimum Storage (page 54)
- Root to Fruit (page 70)
- Love Your Leftovers: Every Last Crumb (page 142), Crying Over Spilled Milk (page 80), Green Salad (page 124)
- Olio app (page 184)

Food Waste – The Elephant in our own Kitchens

It's all too easy to blame big business but, once produce has left the farm gate, 70 per cent of the nation's food waste is generated in our own homes, according to WRAP (The Waste and Resources Action Programme). We are the worst offenders in Europe. It doesn't make any sense; we spend our hard-earned cash on food in order to transport it home, store it and then throw it away.

The great news is that we can all do something about it, with immediate impact, and every positive step we take will make a difference.

It's about saving money as well as saving the planet. The cost of living is soaring, with everyday basics reaching record prices, so it's more important than ever to benefit from every last morsel of the food that we buy. According to WRAP, the average UK family with children threw away around £720 worth of food in 2021 – just think what you could do with that money.

Food Shopping

It may sound rather obvious, but how about buying less to start with? We may all shop in different ways to suit our lifestyles: online, weekly, even daily, but all of us could do with checking our cupboards, fridges and freezers more regularly so that we use up ingredients before replacing them. There's no need to stockpile readily available ingredients; we seem to have a groundless fear of running out of anything nowadays. A morning without breakfast cereal isn't a crisis as long as there's some bread for toast, or perhaps an egg for an omelette. Overbuying leads to waste.

Having a Plan

It doesn't have to be a weekly menu chalked up on the board – it could just be a few pointers scrawled on the back of an envelope – but having a few days of meals mapped out will reduce those spontaneous purchases that often go uneaten.

Some of us cook from precise recipes and may have exact weights and quantities on the shopping list; in those cases, buying loose rather than packaged ingredients can help to reduce the endless half-empty packets of random ingredients left in the cupboard.

When market shopping in particular, it's all about responding to what looks best on the day. There may be a glut of tomatoes to buy cheaply or some gloriously fresh mackerel, but it still pays to have some kind of a meal plan for the next few days. That might be as loose as Monday – curry, Tuesday – grain-based salad, finishing up with a stir-fry on Wednesday to clear the decks.

Make a List and Stick to it

'Bogof' (buy one get one free) offers or multibuys are all too tempting, particularly with perishable food, but so often that second bag of salad is left to fester because you never needed it in the first place. Lists can be prescriptive (with exact weights and quantities), or more vague (potatoes for two meals), according to how you like to cook.

It's so easy to get overexcited in the shops or supermarket. After all, the places are set up to lure you into snapping up those extra treats – so never, ever, go shopping when you're hungry unless you're sure you're going to get through everything you buy! It's so much harder to resist temptation.

Understanding Date Labels

This can save perfectly good food from going in the bin. 'Display until' or 'sell-by' labels are purely for retailers to keep an eye on stock movement and shouldn't concern you at all.

'Use-by' dates are the important ones, as they refer to food safety. You mustn't eat, cook or freeze the product after this date, as it may contain enough harmful bacteria to cause food poisoning. Remember that you can freeze food right up to, and on, the 'use-by' day, even if you're planning on cooking it just a day or two later. If you cook a raw product on its 'use-by' date, it essentially becomes a new product, with a new shelf life.

'Best before' dates are all about quality; according to the producer, or retailer, the food will be at its best before this date, but it is perfectly safe to eat afterwards. This is down to you and your judgement. An egg is a perfect example; it may be past the 'best before' date, but if you crack it and it smells okay, it's fine to use – perhaps not for a poached egg, where freshness is key, but certainly for an omelette.

A stable dried product, such as pasta, will still be safe to eat for years after a 'best before' date, while pulses may take an age to cook after a couple of years and not be quite as nutritious.

It's about using common sense and hopefully, once you're keeping a fairly regular audit of your store cupboard, you'll be unlikely to unearth that ten-year-old can of sardines from the depths of the cupboard one day.

When shopping at independents, or opting for the more sustainable loose vegetables in the supermarket, we have to make our own decisions on whether the food is good to eat. It's what human beings have done for millennia – just a question of smell, sight and touch.

Suppliers of highly perishable goods, such as meat, fish and dairy, will tell you how long they will keep, so maybe keep a note of when you bought them.

Optimum Storage
Your larder, or more likely cupboard, needs to be fairly cool for optimum storage of cans, jars and dried goods. If you refill your own jars with grains and pulses, then keep track of freshness by marking the jar with a date (liquid chalk pens that write on glass are perfect for the job).

A basket, or better still, a rack, is the best place for vegetables that don't like the fridge – such as onions, shallots, garlic and squash.

Potatoes do best in a dark paper bag by themselves, where they are less likely to sprout or turn mouldy (potatoes and onions react with each other, accelerating spoilage, so store them separately).

Many fruits, such as apples, avocados, melons, pears, stone fruit and tomatoes, taste so much better when kept out of the fridge, but do produce ethylene which speeds up ripening and shortens the life of your vegetables. Those old-fashioned, three-tiered vegetable racks, with fruit and vegetables in their own compartments, now make perfect sense.

Bananas produce ethylene too, and are usually best stored in a separate space to prevent them ripening too quickly and spoiling other fruit. You can give a hard melon or pear some help ripening by placing it in a bowl or paper bag with bananas.

The Fridge
This should be kept at 1–5°C/34–41°F to keep your food fresh for longer – particularly when it comes to fish, meat and milk.

A well-organised fridge will reduce waste too. How about a 'last chance and leftovers' shelf for all the bits that need eating first? It's often easier to keep track of leftovers in recycled jars, where you can see the contents at a glance, rather than in random bowls and dishes.

Taking five minutes extra to unload shopping into the fridge can make all the difference; place your new produce at the back, behind more visible and accessible food that you need to use up.

The coldest part of your fridge is the bottom shelf – this is where to store meat, fish, dairy or other foods that spoil quickly.

The 'crisper' drawers, at the bottom of the fridge, are the best place for fruit and vegetables as they maintain more humid conditions for keeping it fresh.

Milk is all too often stored in the fridge door, which is, in fact, the warmest part of the fridge. If you buy more than one bottle, perhaps store the open bottle in the door with your reserves in the bottom compartment of the fridge.

The Freezer
This is your friend (pages 154–157) when it comes to saving leftovers, catching fruit and vegetables on the edge, storing perishable foods and getting into the fabulously sustainable ways of batch cooking. Set it to at least –18°C/0°F.

Winter

IN SEASON

Apples, Beetroots, Brussels Sprouts, Cabbages, Carrots,
Cauliflowers, Celeriac, Celery, Chard, Citrus Fruits, Chicory,
Cranberries, Jerusalem Artichokes, Kale, Nuts, Onions, Parsnips,
Pears, Potatoes, Purple-sprouting Broccoli, Quinces,
Rhubarb, Spring Greens, Squashes, Swedes, Turnips

Eating with the Seasons

Embracing the seasons, as we have done for millennia, is key to eating well for both our own health and our own pleasure, while caring for the world around us.

That tempting punnet of berries sitting on the supermarket shelf in the depths of winter will, most likely, disappoint; the fruit needs to be firm and robust for travel, meaning that it's harvested early, usually before it has developed much taste. The same can be said for imported plums, greengages, raspberries and cherries. A local strawberry in June can be picked at a perfect stage of ripeness, when sugar levels are peaking, ready for immediate sale in the nearby shops. It will smell of summer as you bite into it, and the taste may remind you of childhood – a world apart from its bland, imported cousin that needs to be doused in sugar and sometimes calls for acidity before it's worth eating.

Whether you're talking tomatoes, cucumber, lettuce or asparagus, buying produce in season from smaller local producers is likely to give you a completely different eating experience. Many of the foods that are grown on a huge commercial scale are hybrids, and sadly, flavour and nutrients aren't top of the agenda when they're being developed. Big farming is all about yields, uniformity and shelf life. It's sometimes worth biting into a homegrown tomato just as a reminder; we've become so used to the cotton-wool varieties that are sold year-round in the shops. A few slices of perfectly ripe beefheart tomato on toast with a dash of extra-virgin olive oil and a sprinkling of salt and pepper can be incredibly good. It's worth seeking out and supporting producers growing heritage crops, where taste and quality is everything – otherwise they may disappear.

The 'fresh' imported produce that we can buy year-round is often preserved during long transit and storage times, using gases, sprays and waxes, many containing fungicides and other chemicals that we would probably prefer not to be consuming. Eating with the seasons is about harvesting and celebrating natural food at its best, relishing the freshness and pickling, bottling or freezing during the times of plenty.

When it comes to health, intense tastes and flavours are often signals that a food is at its best, bursting with vitamins, minerals and nutrients. Once picked, fresh produce begins to degrade; it no longer has the ground, or tree, as its source of nutrients and energy. Vitamin C is particularly vulnerable to oxygen and light, and despite all the modern technology involved in cold storage, nutrient levels do reduce with time.

The natural availability of certain ingredients at different times of year links into the rhythm of life. Comforting soups and stews of root vegetables with warming spices help to sustain us through cold, dark days, while crisp salads of radishes, cucumbers and leaves are refreshing and rehydrating in hotter weather. Celebrating events or holidays with particular seasonal ingredients creates food memories and traditions to look forward to. You might have an annual asparagus feast for a birthday, a strawberry

pavlova at dusk on the summer solstice, pumpkin quesadillas for Halloween or forced rhubarb tart on Valentine's Day. Anticipating and looking forward to seasonal food reminds us that eating is anything but humdrum and repetitive: it's a pleasure to be savoured and shared.

Seasonal Shopping is Better for the Environment

Transporting food around the world comes at a cost, particularly if we're talking about planes. Flying our food imports, rather than shipping or driving them, costs the planet substantially more. It's hard to quantify, and statistics vary, showing between 50 and 100 times the carbon emissions for airfreight over other forms of transport. It's time to start moving away from highly perishable goods such as green beans, asparagus and berries that are flown around the globe. It's time to take action; we should demand that companies have to label food that has been airfreighted, giving us informed choices. Meanwhile, it's a question of detective work.

When we talk about seasonality, and particularly in relation to fruit, we're often referring to European produce as well as our own. Our temperate climate is rather limiting and a cook's life without lemons would be depressing. The Mediterranean citrus season makes a welcome arrival in the depths of winter, along with Father Christmas. Boxes of clementines and tissue-wrapped blood oranges provide the perfect zing and zest to fight off seasonal snuffles. The summer stone fruit season is one to look forward to, and while we can buy fabulous local cherries and plums, we rely upon Spanish and Italian apricots, nectarines and peaches. We need to engage with our food and use some common sense – regularly tucking in to local apples, because they grow on our doorstep, while enjoying the occasional Turkish fig because we don't have the climate for them.

Fish, meat and dairy have their seasons too, and good specialist suppliers and shopkeepers will keep you informed. Fish move with ocean currents and sea temperatures, making certain species locally available at particular times of the year. There are also periods when they should be left to spawn and rebuild stocks if we hope to eat fish in the future. Meat, such as lamb, is seasonal too, with a high demand at Easter but an often more flavoursome joint, at a much better price, in late summer. There's also the game season, when you can sometimes pick up your supper cheaply, or find venison that is hunted to control numbers in an attempt to maintain the balance of nature. Some cheeses are seasonal, with rich milk from pasture-fed animals giving gloriously fresh cheeses in spring and summer, and more mature cheeses, such as wonderful blue Stilton, in the winter months.

Reconnecting with nature, with our producers and our suppliers, is the most wonderful way to punctuate the year with seasonal treats; better for us and better for the planet, it's a win-win.

Jerusalem Artichoke Soup

Jerusalem artichokes are an absolute joy in the winter, tasting like an indulgent treat without a fat price tag. These little tubers do wonders for your health too, as they're loaded with starchy fibre that gives your gut bacteria a feast. The only downside can be some fairly windy repercussions if you consume large quantities; preparing tiny glasses or espresso-sized cups of this soup as a taster to serve with drinks, or as an appetiser, is the fail-safe option.

SERVES 4, OR 12 DEMI-TASSE PORTIONS

40g (1½oz) butter
4 banana shallots, diced
2 celery sticks, finely sliced
2 garlic cloves, crushed
500g (1lb 2oz) Jerusalem artichokes
Dash of lemon juice or cider or white wine vinegar (optional)
1 litre (1¾ pints) chicken or vegetable stock
3–4 tbsp double cream
20g (¾oz) Parmesan cheese, finely grated
3 tbsp parsley oil, to garnish (page 64)
Salt and pepper

Heat the butter in a large saucepan over a low heat and fry the shallots and celery for at least 10 minutes until soft. Add the garlic and cook until you really catch its aroma.

Your artichokes can be peeled for a perfect white cream or, if you're happy with a slightly speckled appearance, can be well scrubbed and cooked with the skin on. Chop the artichokes into rough chunks and, if preparing in advance, store in water with a dash of lemon juice or vinegar to prevent them from browning.

Add the artichokes, stock and a pinch of salt to the pan and cook for 30 minutes, or until the artichokes begin to break down.

Blend the soup with a hand-held blender until smooth and silky and, if serving in tiny glasses or cups, strain it too. Add the cream, Parmesan and salt and pepper to taste. Divide among bowls or cups and garnish the soup with a swirl of parsley oil.

TRY THIS
- Halving the amount of stock and serving as a purée with pan-fried, diver-caught scallops.
- Roasting well-scrubbed artichokes (take care to remove any grit) in a hot oven with a dash of olive oil, lemon juice and a few sprigs of thyme.

Creamed Vegetable Soup

There's nothing more comforting than a bowl of soup in the depths of winter. Once you have mastered this technique you'll make soups with your eyes closed, varying the vegetables with what you happen to have in store. Soup bases make excellent purées or sauces to serve with grains, pulses or roasted vegetables too.

SERVES 4

50g (1¾oz) butter or 50ml (2fl oz) extra-virgin olive oil
2 onions, finely chopped
2 garlic cloves, crushed
800g (1lb 12oz) root vegetables or squash, plus 200g (7oz) potato for a thicker, heartier soup, roughly chopped
Any spices, grated zest, dried herbs of choice
100ml (3½fl oz) dry sherry, white wine, white vermouth or 2 tbsp white wine vinegar and a splash of water
1 litre (1¾ pints) vegetable or chicken stock
Lemon or lime juice or splash of sherry vinegar
Any optional dairy, such as cream, yogurt or crème fraîche, or oat cream or nut butter
Any fresh herbs
Any pestos or extra toppings (see pages 92 and 93)
Salt and pepper

Here's your template:

Heat the butter or oil in a large saucepan over a medium heat and fry the onions for 10 minutes, or until softened. Add the garlic and cook for a further 2 minutes until you're engulfed in the aroma.

Add your vegetables to the pan with any spices and herbs and fry for 1 minute, then add the alcohol or vinegar and 200ml (7fl oz) of the stock. Cover and simmer until the vegetables are tender – about 15 minutes, depending on the size of your chunks. Top up with a little more stock if the pan is getting dry.

Blitz the vegetables with a hand-held blender; this is the stage to stop and freeze your soup base, if you like, or to season and serve the purée as a thick sauce, or you can add the rest of the stock to make your soup. Season with salt, pepper, citrus and add any dairy, herbs and extra toppings before serving.

See opposite for variations.

CARROT AND GINGER SOUP

SERVES 4

- Carrot
- 1 tsp ground cumin
- 1 tbsp grated fresh root ginger
- 1 tsp grated orange zest

Season with:
- Orange juice and a dash of lime juice
- A swirl of yogurt
- A few coriander leaves

SPICED PARSNIP SOUP

SERVES 4

- Parsnip
- 1 grated Bramley apple
- 1 tbsp medium curry powder

Season with:
- 1 tsp black mustard seeds, a pinch of chilli flakes and 8 curry leaves fried for 2 minutes (see page 46)
- Lime juice and grated zest
- A swirl of yogurt

CELERIAC AND HAZELNUT SOUP

SERVES 4

- Celeriac and butter beans (2:1)
- 1 bay leaf

Season with:
- Lemon juice
- A spoonful of cream
- A sprinkle of dill
- Chopped roasted hazelnuts

SQUASH AND ROSEMARY SOUP

SERVES 4

- Squash
- 2 tsp finely chopped fresh rosemary

Season with:
- Lemon juice and grated zest
- Grated Parmesan
- Toasted pumpkin seeds

Soup Toppings

Garnishes aren't just about appearances, they can add the magic touch of texture, a contrasting flavour, some indulgent creaminess or a flash of zingy acidity that makes the soup extra special.

A bit of crunch is often welcome. Try sprinkling roasted nuts, toasted seeds (page 28), crispy bacon, pickles (page 47) or you could try these:

Quick Croutons
Toast 2 slices of stale bread. Rub the toast with ½ garlic clove, drizzle with olive oil and cut into squares. Tumble the squares in grated Parmesan or nutritional yeast and sprinkle over your soup just before serving.

Herb Oils
Root vegetables are often sweet and earthy tasting, so a fresh herbaceous oil makes a good contrast. Oils are a great way to make the most of a surplus of soft herbs, such as basil, dill, parsley, coriander and tarragon. The vibrant green oil keeps its colour for at least a week in the fridge.

To make a herb oil, blanch the herbs in simmering water for about 2 minutes, then refresh in ice-cold water. Pick off the leaves, dab them dry and add to a blender with your chosen oil (about 10g/¼oz herbs to 100ml/3½fl oz oil). Olive oil works well for Mediterranean flavours, but sunflower oil will be a better match for other cuisines. Blitz the herbs and oil, then strain through a coffee filter or muslin-lined sieve. Store in the fridge for up to a week.

A Touch of Fat
A swirl of yogurt, cream, crème fraîche or soured cream can make soup taste more indulgent, and if you're opting for a dairy-free alternative, then think of rich additions such as coconut milk, coconut yogurt, a pesto or a few spoonfuls of whipped tahini.

To make a whipped tahini, blend or whisk together equal quantities of tahini and water, then add lemon juice and season to taste. You may like to add crushed garlic, roasted garlic or herbs to the tahini too.

A Splash of Acidity
When it comes to acidity it's hard to beat a dash of citrus juice, but some vinegars such as sherry vinegar or balsamic vinegar could be delicious too. Meanwhile, a small sprinkling of chopped preserved lemon, sauerkraut or kimchi will add both an interesting sharpness and savouriness.

Tangy grated apple or perhaps a handful of pomegranate seeds can also give some welcome piquancy to a creamy soup.

Other Ways to Add Interest
Finely shredded greens, such as Brussels sprouts, kale or cabbage, can be stir-fried with a spoonful of olive oil and some crushed garlic, grated fresh root ginger or finely chopped chilli pepper, depending on the flavour of your soup.

Minestrone

Minestrone, the Italian 'Big Soup', is the perfect way to enjoy a huge variety of seasonal vegetables in one meal and use up any random bits. How about instituting Minestrone Mondays – a weekly clear-out of the vegetable basket? This soup is substantial and loaded with protein with the addition of beans and pasta or sometimes rice, but there's nothing to stop you adding pearl barley or buckwheat; you're the boss.

SERVES 6–8

3 tbsp olive oil
1 onion, diced
2 carrots, diced
2 celery sticks, diced
500g (1lb 2oz) peeled and diced vegetables, such as squash, celeriac or parsnips
2 potatoes, diced into 2–3cm (¾–1¼ inch) pieces
1 large stem of rosemary, finely chopped
A piece of Parmesan rind (optional, see note below)
2 litres (3½ pints) vegetable stock (or chicken stock for a richer result)
400g (14oz) can borlotti beans (or any whole pulse of choice)
100g (3½oz) broken-up wholewheat or spelt pasta or tiny pasta shapes, such as ditalini
200g (7oz) Swiss chard or kale or other seasonal greens
Freshly grated Parmesan, lemon juice, salt, pepper and extra-virgin olive oil, to serve

Heat the olive oil in a large saucepan over a medium heat and cook the onion, carrots and celery for 10 minutes, or until softened. Add the diced vegetables and potatoes, stirring them into the oil and cooking for a further 2 minutes. Add the rosemary and Parmesan rind (if using).

Pour the stock into the pan and simmer until the potatoes are starting to soften. Add the beans and pasta and simmer until the pasta is just about cooked.

Now add the greens, stripped of any tough stalks and shredded into bite-sized pieces and bubble for 1–2 minutes. Balance the soup with Parmesan, lemon juice, salt, pepper and a drizzle of extra-virgin olive oil to serve.

TRY THIS
- Keep Parmesan cheese rind and next time you are making minestrone or risotto, add it in one piece with the stock. Don't forget to remove it before serving as it will have done its work enriching and flavouring the dish.
- Spaghetti can be snapped into tiny pieces for soups, while short pasta is best bashed with a rolling pin to create irregular shards – a good way to finish off any random packets you may have.
- During the summer substitute the celeriac and pumpkin with green beans, peas and courgettes; add a little diced tomato, replace the rosemary with parsley and top with a fragrant pesto. Just add your delicate vegetables at the same point you would add the greens. Minestrone is definitely a moveable feast.

Eat More Veg

There's now more nutritional and dietary advice available to us than ever before. We demonise a food group one year and put it back on the menu the next. There are miracle weight-loss diets, muscle-building formulas, paths to longevity and recipes to boost our energy and mood. The one constant – the one thing our health experts all seem to agree upon – is that eating a wide range of vegetables is good for us.

According to recent research, despite all the noise around the five-a-day campaign, less than 30 per cent of the under 65s and fewer than one in ten of our children are currently reaching that target. That's pretty dismal news; it's time to drop the stick and embrace the carrot, in every sense.

Once we celebrate the true wonders of vegetables – how tasty they can be, how economical they are when chosen wisely and how versatile they are to prepare – then we can also relish the fact that they're loaded with fibre, vitamins and nutrients as an added, very substantial, bonus.

If you are following a vegetarian or vegan diet, make sure to combine your vegetables with plenty of grains and pulses so that you're consuming enough protein. Vitamin C is crucial to effectively absorb iron from plant sources, so a pile of greens and a welcome squeeze of citrus juice not only freshens up a bowl of lentils or quinoa, but it increases your iron intake as well.

Rather than obsessing over this month's superfood, seeking out dark green leaves for their high vitamin K and folate content or buying orange pumpkins for their vitamin A, it's really a question of variety. The nutritionist's mantra, 'Eat the Rainbow', may seem simplistic, but it's sound advice; cast the net wide and you will be packing in a broad spectrum of nutrients and the fibre that so many of us are lacking in our diets. Vegetables no longer just mean potato and peas, or the odd bit of broccoli playing second fiddle to meat; there are hundreds of exciting varieties to try and so many ways to make them the stars of the show.

It's true to say that vegetables are unlikely to top most children's desert island dinner menu. Green vegetables are often bitter, and even more so to a young palate. As hunter-gatherers we evolved to be wary of bitterness, as many toxins are bitter, so it may take a while to learn to love them. It's all about exposure (page 119) and about serving vegetables numerous times, even when rejected.

In this book there are many recipes where vegetables take centre stage, but it's also worth remembering how wonderful natural vegetables can taste too. A grated carrot salad with just lemon juice, extra-virgin olive oil and some seasoning is a perfect example.

A great way of increasing your plant uptake is to snack on raw vegetables before a meal, when you are at your hungriest. How about a picking platter with a selection of vegetables, some fruit, nuts and seeds and a dip (pages 40–41 and 131)? You may be amazed at how everyone tucks in, and any leftovers can end up in a salad, soup or stir-fry.

Root to Fruit

While a lot of domestic food waste is down to items going off, or being thrown out because they're deemed to be past their best, we also needlessly throw out so many vegetable tops and trimmings, rinds and skins that are packed with nutrients and flavour.

The concept of 'root to fruit' is that, once we've harvested a fruit or vegetable, we should make the most of every scrap.

Peelings Can be Made into Crisps
Beetroot, carrot, parsnip and potato peelings can be tossed with a little oil and salt, spread out over a roasting tray and baked in an oven preheated to 180°C/160°C fan/gas 4 for about 10–15 minutes until crisp. Turn them after 5 minutes and watch them as they may burn. Cool on a wire rack.

Brassica Stalks are Fabulously Crisp
Cabbage cores, broccoli and cauliflower stalks can all be stir-fried or served in a salad. Slice off the dry fibrous ends and, if needed, peel away any tough outer skin before slicing as finely as possible.

Tender Herb Stalks Can be Added to Soups, Stews and Dressings
Parsley, coriander and basil stalks can all be finely chopped and used alongside the leaves.

Trimmings Make Great Stock
Carrot, celery, leek, onion and parsley offcuts make great traditional stock (page 102). Fennel stalks, asparagus stumps, tomato skins and mushroom trimmings give more distinctive flavours to stock, so be aware of your end dish. The tough outer leaves of lemongrass will add a lovely Southeast-Asian aroma to a stock. Empty pea and broad bean pods are filled with flavour, which can provide the base for a soup or risotto.

What to leave out? Potatoes will cloud a stock and add little flavour. Meanwhile, parsnips, turnips and brassicas will overpower the flavours

and you'll be in danger of creating that pervasive 1970s school, boiled-to-hell, veg smell – never appealing.

Potatoes Are the Most Wasted Veg of the Lot
We throw away almost half of the potatoes that we grow in this country. Storing at cool room temperature in a dark, ventilated place – a cloth bag or paper sack is ideal – will preserve your potatoes for longer. If your potatoes have sprouted a few little 'eyes' or developed the odd green patch they are still edible; just remove them and use the rest of the potato. However, don't eat potatoes once they've turned completely green.

Parboiled potatoes can be frozen, and then roasted from frozen for super roasties. The odd leftover potato can also be finely chopped and added to soups and stews where it will collapse and thicken the liquid beautifully.

Root vegetables often come with leaves attached (it's a great sign that they are super fresh), so, after buying, chop the leaves off so that they do not sap the roots of moisture – and use them quickly (your roots will keep for longer).

You can cook beetroot tops just as you would spinach or chard (see Steam-fried Greens, page 73).

Carrot tops are loaded with vitamins and have a slightly bitter taste that works well in sweet-and-sour vinaigrettes and pestos (pages 125 and 92).

Celery and celeriac leaves are delicious used raw or cooked, in the same way you'd use parsley. Tough stalks or stems are perfect for making stock.

Leek and spring onion tops are perfectly edible; tougher outer leaves are great for stock, while the tender greens can be finely chopped and used alongside the rest of the root (they take longer to soften if cooking, so add a little extra time).

Radish leaves are often too fuzzy to eat in a salad, but great in a pesto or cooked briefly like spinach.

Turnip tops are prized in many other countries, and they're loaded with calcium. As the leaves become older and bigger they become more bitter, so go for younger leaves if possible (see Steam-fried Greens, page 73).

Leftover cooked potatoes can be mashed and fried as potato cakes, fishcakes (even with canned fish) or added to Bubble and Squeak (page 100), as can leftover roast potatoes. Don't leave a lone potato in your vegetable basket; cook it with the rest and use it up with other leftovers.

Leftover chip-shop chips make the most fabulous Spanish tortilla. Just fry some onions in olive oil until golden while you chop some chips. Mix the onions and chopped chips with about an equal volume of well-seasoned, beaten eggs in a large bowl and cook in a well-oiled frying pan over a low heat until beginning to set. You can turn the omelette onto a plate and slip it back in to fry the other side or just grill the top side to make things easier. Your tortilla is cooked as soon as it has just firmed up. Eat hot or cold.

Veg on the Edge

That slightly bendy carrot or tired leaf of spinach will still be tasty in a soup (pages 62–63). Try to have a vegetable sweep at least once a week where everything finishes up in a Minestrone (page 67), curry, being roasted or, at the very least, prepped and frozen for another day.

The last resort is the compost bin (see pages 106–107) where your vegetable scraps will rejoin the cycle of life, feeding back into the soil ecosystem that we rely on to feed us, rather than festering in landfill and creating methane.

Steam-fried Greens

'Eat your greens' is a mantra that so often seems to fall on deaf ears; here's a cooking method to turn things around. It's super versatile and can work as a side or as the star of the show.

Banish all memories of the sulphurous school cabbage and embrace this simple way with leaves. It's as successful with the tightly packed leaves of cabbages such as Savoy, hispi or spring greens as it is with the loose leaves of kale, chard or even beet, turnip or kohlrabi tops.

SERVES 4

400–500g (14oz–1lb 2oz) cabbage or other greens
2 tbsp oil, such as olive, rapeseed, sunflower or a 50/50 mix of butter and oil
2 garlic cloves, crushed
120ml (4fl oz) white wine or white vermouth
Salt and pepper

Cut the cabbage in half through the core and shred as finely as possible, leaving behind only the tough part of the stem. If you are using loose leaves such as kale or chard, pull the leaf away from the stem and roughly chop, then slice across the stalks into small chunks and keep separate. Wash your greens thoroughly, as organic vegetables can contain the odd slug! Drain, but don't worry if the leaves are still damp.

Heat the oil in a large frying or sauté pan, add any stalks or stems (the pan should be hot enough that they sizzle), and stir-fry for about 1 minute. Add all the greens and fry until the pan has dried up and they just begin to brown.

Toss in a pinch of salt and the garlic, then, as soon as you smell the garlic (and this will be a matter of seconds), pour in the wine. Stir until the moisture has evaporated. Serve with a good grind of black pepper.

MAKING A MEAL OF IT

- Top with a poached egg, some fried tofu or crumbled cheese and serve on top of a pile of cooked whole grains or pulses.
- Serve on top of dal (page 44) with a dollop of yogurt.

Variations

Soy, ginger, sesame oil + seeds. Just add soy sauce, a dash of rice wine vinegar and water instead of the wine, ginger along with the garlic and a drop of toasted sesame oil and seeds to serve.

Soft cooking chorizo, fino sherry + sultanas + chickpeas. Fry the sliced chorizo for 2 minutes before adding your greens, then add sherry instead of the wine and stir in sultanas and chickpeas to warm through and serve.

Chilli, lemon + Parmesan. Add chilli flakes to the pan with the garlic, and season with lemon juice and finely grated zest. Serve with a sprinkling of grated Parmesan. Perfect with Socca (page 112).

Rainbow Slaw

A fresh, crunchy salad makes such a welcome contrast to traditional, hearty winter food. Slaws are a brilliant way to consume an entire rainbow of fruit and vegetables, boosting immunity levels just when we need to fight off all the seasonal illnesses.

Here's an opportunity to use up any random vegetable to serve with a baked potato or an omelette, and any leftovers keep perfectly for a lunchbox the following day.

SERVES 4

½ red onion, diced
150g (5oz) red cabbage or white or hispi cabbage or Brussels sprouts, finely sliced
2 carrots (heritage carrots look beautiful), cut into small chunks, matchsticks or discs
100g (3½oz) celeriac, kohlrabi, cauliflower, parsnip or beetroot, cut into small chunks, matchsticks or discs (finely slice any cauliflower cores)
1 apple or pear, unpeeled, cored and cut into chunks
4 dates, finely chopped, or dried figs, raisins or sultanas
A handful of nuts, such as walnuts, hazelnuts, almonds or peanuts
2 tbsp toasted seeds, such as sunflower, pumpkin, sesame, flax, hemp or ßpoppy
A handful of fresh mint, parsley or coriander leaves (optional)

Dressing
2 tbsp vinegar (play around with your favourite cider, sherry or wine vinegar)
4 tbsp extra-virgin olive oil
1 tsp Dijon or grainy mustard
Salt and pepper

Place all the chopped vegetables and fruit in a large bowl and add the dried fruit, nuts, seeds and herbs (if using).

Shake the dressing ingredients together in a jar, balancing with salt and pepper. Don't worry about sweetness, as you have plenty of fruit in the slaw. Toss everything together immediately before any fruit or vegetables begin to oxidise and turn brown.

The slaw can sit happily for a couple of days and is best eaten at room temperature.

TRY THIS
Add 2 tsp grated fresh root ginger, 1 tsp toasted sesame oil and 1 tbsp miso paste to the dressing for a zippy Asian take.

Cabbage and Parmesan Slaw
Fantastically simple and astoundingly good, try this with Brussels sprouts too. Very finely shred about 400g (14oz) white or hispi cabbage. Add the juice of a lemon and 1 tsp finely grated zest. Grate over 2 tbsp Parmesan cheese and toss with 3 tbsp extra-virgin olive oil. Add black pepper or Urfa chilli flakes, to taste (the cheese should provide enough saltiness).

Less Meat

We all have choice when we shop, and that choice will be guided by our upbringing, our habits and our budget. While more and more of us are concerned about global warming and worry about the plunging numbers of plant species, birds and insects, we often don't think about it as we plan our weekly menus.

More than a third of all man-made greenhouse gas emissions are generated by agriculture and, added to that, farming is the biggest driver of habitat loss and by far the greatest consumer of fresh water on the planet. The food we choose to buy, where it comes from and how it has been produced is one of the most impactful decisions we can make when it comes to our future. It's increasingly evident that the growing demand for meat, alongside a growing world population, is not sustainable, and we all have a part to play. Despite the fact that meat consumption is beginning to decline in Britain, we still eat almost double the global average.

Across the globe, three-quarters of our farmed land is used to graze livestock, or to grow crops to feed livestock, and yet under a fifth of our calories come from livestock and dairy consumption. Conservationists point out that we could feed the world if we used land more efficiently, by growing more protein-rich plants such as pulses for human consumption, and that this would allow us to rewild much of the overgrazed land.

When it comes to emissions, vast areas of land, and natural forest in particular, are being cleared globally to grow crops to feed livestock, releasing carbon from the trees and soil into the atmosphere. Ruminants such as cattle and sheep release methane as they digest, as well as when their manure decays. With over a billion of each on the planet, that is a lot of methane.

Water consumption may not be a top priority in Britain, but, globally, water scarcity is a massive concern. Beef tops UNESCO's table when it comes to its 'water print', requiring over 15,000 litres of water to produce a kilo of meat – compared with just over 4,000 litres for a kilo of pulses. On a protein count, beef fared even worse, requiring 112 litres per gram of protein in comparison with pulses' 19 litres per gram of protein. While we may not yet be so concerned with water consumption in the UK, one thing that has been hitting the headlines is the dire state of our rivers. There's no doubt that excessive quantities of chicken manure, along with cattle and pig slurry being spread on our fields from the growing number of factory or 'mega' farms, is taking its toll.

There are many different angles to take when assessing which type of meat production is more costly to the planet; overall scientists agree that red meat, and particularly beef and lamb (and dairy) are the biggest problem. When you choose to eat meat, sourcing local, pasture-fed animals is important.

And what about chicken? Nowadays we eat around a billion birds a year. A staggering 95 per cent of British chicken is raised in intensive indoor units, making it cheaper for the consumer, but detrimental to animal welfare and the environment. It may be tempting to buy that bargain supermarket chicken for less than a pint in the pub, but surely it's better to splash out on more sustainably sourced chicken that meets welfare standards, if we can afford to, and make eating chicken an occasional treat?

Here lies the core of the discussion. Continuous pressure from our retailers and food industry has led to 'affordable' meat, but at what cost? Intensive farms, where animal welfare is an afterthought and where imported feed leaves a disastrous footprint, have given us plentiful cheap and – let's be honest – rather tasteless meat.

Better Meat

Britain is pretty rugged in places, and it's wet. We have swathes of marginal land that is far more suited to livestock than arable farming. We also have many farmers who have turned, or are in the process of turning, their backs on intensive agriculture and are now farming with nature.

Regenerative farming, where the focus is on rebuilding living soils and healing the land, is dependent on ruminants. Livestock are part of this holistic approach to looking after the land; as they graze, they trample down plants, creating a protective thatch over the soil, and their dung deposits nutrients back into the land, feeding soil biodiversity and growing more grass. These grazing lands become carbon sinks which provide habitat and food for wildlife.

Pasture-fed meat costs more, but we have to value the extra time, the land management, the smaller abattoirs and the local butchers. Land use for pasture-fed meat is much greater than more intensive, industrial farming systems, and this method of rearing livestock can't satisfy the growing global appetite for animal protein. Remember, too, that pasture-fed livestock, especially beef cattle, often grazes species-rich fields, important habitats that need grazing cattle to maintain. We therefore have to choose our meat carefully and eat less of it.

Buying much less but much better meat makes sense on every level. There's no feeling of deprivation if you choose to use small amounts of well-flavoured meat cleverly – to add depth of flavour to a dish or as a fabulous garnish, rather than thinking that it needs to be the main player. The occasional Sunday roast (page 97) becomes a treat to look forward to.

So much about the way we eat is habit, but habits can and do change. The traditional meat-and-two-veg is being replaced by a much more exciting, diverse menu with a multitude of wonderful global influences. Even if you have a taste for traditional comfort food, you can eke out the meat in a stew with some pulses and grains (page 79).

'Eke out the Meat', Beef Stew

Stew is a wonderfully warming winter dish where a small amount of meat can feed a crowd. Key to this recipe is getting enough umami (that savoury depth) into the dish so that it feels rich and satisfying. The mushrooms and anchovies will work their magic while the herb and olive paste adds a fresh zippiness at the end.

SERVES 6–8

- 10g (¼oz) dried porcini mushrooms
- 200ml (7fl oz) boiling water
- 1 tbsp plain flour
- 1 tbsp mustard powder
- 500g (1lb 2oz) chuck steak, cut into large chunks
- 3 tbsp olive oil
- 1 large onion, diced
- 2 carrots, diced
- 2 celery sticks, diced
- 200g (7oz) portobello, cremini or shiitake mushrooms, roughly chopped
- 6 canned anchovies, roughly chopped
- 2 tbsp tomato purée
- 150ml (5fl oz) red wine
- 1 bay leaf
- 1 tbsp finely chopped fresh rosemary or thyme leaves (or a mixture)
- 500ml (17fl oz) beef stock
- 300g (10½oz) vegetables, such as celeriac, pumpkin, parsnip, turnip or swede, diced
- 100g (3½oz) pearl barley
- 2 x 400g (14oz) cans beans, such as butter beans, haricot beans, borlotti or cannelloni, drained (or about 400–500g/14oz–1lb 2oz home-cooked)
- Salt and pepper
- Brown rice, jacket potatoes and Steam-fried Greens (page 73), to serve (optional)

Herb and olive seasoning
- A handful of fresh parsley
- 10 green olives
- 1 large garlic clove
- Finely grated zest and juice of ½ lemon

Soak the porcini mushrooms in the boiling water.

Meanwhile, spread the flour and mustard powder out on a plate, mix together, then toss the meat in the seasoned flour. Heat half the olive oil in a large casserole dish and sear the meat (in two batches if necessary) until well browned. Remove the meat from the pan and set aside.

Add the onion, carrots, celery and fresh mushrooms to the pan with the remaining oil and fry over a medium heat for 15 minutes, or until the onion has softened and the mushrooms have collapsed.

Drain the porcini, reserving the stock, and chop roughly. Add the porcini and its stock, the anchovies, tomato purée, wine, bay leaf, herbs, a pinch of salt and pepper and beef stock and simmer gently for 2 hours. Alternatively, cook in an oven preheated to 160°C/140°C fan/gas 3.

After 2 hours, add the root vegetables and pearl barley and cook for a further 1 hour, or until the meat is beautifully tender.

Roughly chop all the ingredients for the herb seasoning and add most of this mixture to the stew together with the beans, then allow to heat through for about 10 minutes. Check the seasoning, sprinkle with the remaining herb seasoning and enjoy as a one-pot supper or serve with brown rice, jacket potatoes and maybe some Steam-fried Greens.

TRY THIS
- Beef shin is a great cut of meat for this dish; if using, just add another hour to the cooking time.
- How about cooking this in a slow cooker or pressure cooker to reduce the energy consumption?

Crying Over Spilled Milk

The age-old expression 'there's no use crying over spilled milk' may be true metaphorically, but thinking about the vast quantity of milk that goes down the drain every day in the UK really is enough to make you weep. Milk is the third most wasted food item in our homes after potatoes (page 70) and bread (page 142); according to WRAP (The Waste and Resources Action Programme) we literally pour away almost 500 million pints of milk in this country per year. Milk waste is harmful down our drains because of its high 'oxygen demand'. Bacteria that feed on it use up oxygen that would otherwise be used by aquatic life in the water course. It is classified as a 'difficult' waste.

So What Can We Do About It?

We can preserve our milk for longer. Many household fridges aren't turned down to the optimum 5°C/41°F. Added to that, most people keep milk in the fridge door where temperatures are at their highest. Lower temperatures will extend the life of pretty much anything in the fridge; perhaps while you keep the open milk in the door, you can store any extra milk in the cool bottom drawer.

Milk is often drinkable well past its use-by date; it's about having a sniff, or a tiny sample, before making any decisions. There is nothing dangerous about slightly sour milk; it's just a matter of taste. Sour milk makes an ideal cooking ingredient, as it's perfect for scones, soda bread and cornbread. You could also consider using it to make a batch of cheese sauce for a mac and cheese.

Milk 'on the edge' can make a brilliant ricotta-style cheese. The extra tanginess actually adds flavour. Homemade ricotta would be wonderful in a galette (pages 164–165) or spread on toast and topped with fresh greens or fruit.

Remember to recycle your milk containers appropriately (page 180).

HOMEMADE 'RICOTTA'

MAKES ABOUT 200G (7OZ)

- 600ml (1 pint) full-fat milk
- ½–1 tsp salt
- 2 tbsp lemon juice or white wine vinegar

Heat the milk and salt in a large saucepan until almost boiling; you'll see the froth begin to rise, but be careful not to let it boil over. Stir in the lemon juice or vinegar and remove the pan from the heat. Leave the milk to stand for about 10 minutes, allowing the curds to split from the whey, then strain through a muslin-lined sieve for 45 minutes for a soft ricotta and 2–3 hours for a firmer texture. Store the cheese in an airtight container in the fridge for up to 5 days. The leftover liquid whey can be used in baking or even for watering your plants.

Overcatering – Freeze, Please Louise

If you have bought too much milk you can freeze it successfully. Be sure to remove a little milk from the bottle so that it doesn't split the container as it expands. Milk will often separate and look a little lumpy as it thaws, so shake it well and it will come back together. A slightly yellow discolouration often occurs but it doesn't affect the flavour.

When it comes to cheese, savouring small quantities of artisan cheese rather than thinking of cheese as a default snacking ingredient or sandwich filler is a good way to reduce consumption. If you do have too much then:

- Remember to use up any odd nubbly bits of cheese by grating them for toasted sandwiches.

- Parmesan rind is perfect added to a soup or stock for extra flavour.

- Random bits of soft cheeses can be whipped into a dip with yogurt and herbs.

Milk: The Choice is Yours

Over the last few years milk prices have plunged, pushing some smaller farmers out of the business while mega farms are on the increase. Buying milk, cheese and other dairy products from select producers or farms, choosing organic or opting for milk from pasture-fed cows, are ways of supporting higher animal welfare and more sustainable farming practices.

You may also find a local farm shop, deli or store with a milk dispensing machine where you can refill glass milk bottles, reducing the vast numbers of plastic milk cartons that we discard every day (which should always be recycled). The popularity of milk deliveries is back on the rise. It's all about doing a bit of research and deciding what works for you.

Just as we are all being advised to reduce our meat consumption because of the impact, particularly of cattle, on greenhouse gas emissions (page 51), we are also encouraged to reduce our dairy intake.

According to a University of Oxford study, plant milks, when compared litre for litre with dairy, produce about a third of the greenhouse gas emissions, require a fraction of the water and a tiny proportion of the land to produce.

Plant Milks

Our shops are packed with dairy alternatives nowadays, each with a different flavour and nutrient profile, and each with a different 'food print'. Since dairy has been such an important source of calcium in western diets, many of the plant milks available are fortified with calcium along with vitamins (B12 in particular, which is hard to source in vegan diets).

Here in northern Europe it makes sense to embrace oat milk, which wins in sustainability rankings. We grow plenty of oats (in fact, well over half wind up in animal feed). There are also plenty of oat creams, spreads and yogurts on the market.

Soya milk gets some bad press, as we hear about swathes of the Amazon being cut down for soy production. But, according to The World Wildlife Fund, up to 80 per cent of the soya grown globally is used to feed livestock. Most soya milk available in the UK is actually made from European-grown soya and is considered one of the most sustainable and high-protein dairy alternatives.

Hemp and flax milks are becoming more widely available. They rely on niche crops rather than huge monocultures and so help to increase agricultural diversity.

If you're after a nut milk then hazelnuts, which can grow in cooler, wetter climates, are more sustainable than almonds.

Coconut milk, rice milk, cashew milk, pea milk... there are so many options. Perhaps variety is the best approach, as each provides a different set of nutrients.

Leek and Pumpkin Speltotto with Crumbled Blue Cheese

Comfort food as it begins to get colder. Use pearled spelt, rather than the more robust whole grain, to create the soft, slightly chewy texture. The pumpkin is all about creating a creamy mouthfeel as it collapses into the dish. You could even use the leftovers from a Halloween jack-o'-lantern.

SERVES 4

3 medium leeks, trimmed
1 litre (1¾ pints) vegetable stock or chicken stock
2 tbsp extra-virgin olive oil
40g (1½oz) butter
200g (7oz) peeled and diced squash or pumpkin
2 garlic cloves, crushed
4 sprigs of thyme, leaves picked
300g (10½oz) pearled spelt
200ml (7fl oz) dry white wine or white vermouth
200g (7oz) Stilton or any other hard blue cheese, rind removed
A generous handful of fresh parsley, roughly chopped
Salt and pepper

Chop the leeks into 2cm (¾ inch) slices, making sure to wash away any grit. Place any leek trimmings into the stock and bring the stock to a low simmer.

Warm through the olive oil and butter in large saucepan over a medium heat, add the leek slices, squash, garlic and thyme leaves and stir for about 10 minutes. The idea is to soften them, rather than brown them.

Add the spelt and stir with the vegetables before pouring in the wine. Bring to the boil, and then once the liquid has disappeared, get ready to add the stock. Discard the leek trimmings, then ladle in the stock in 3 batches, stirring the contents of the pan over a medium heat, and waiting for the liquid to be absorbed before adding the next ladle. Your grains will be tender, with a bit more bite than a traditional rice risotto, after about 25–30 minutes.

Crumble in half of the cheese, stir and season with a little salt and plenty of pepper before sprinkling with the remaining cheese and the parsley.

TRY THIS
- Use pearl barley in place of the spelt.
- Not a great fan of blue cheese? Top with Parmesan, goat's cheese or even warm hummus.
- Sprinkle with walnuts or roasted almonds.

Chocolate and Rum Prune Pudding

A simple, batter pudding along the lines of the classic French clafoutis. You can omit the chocolate and use fresh stone fruits instead of the prunes for a more traditional version, if you like, but this combination makes a wonderful winter treat. Best eaten warm and served with a dollop of yogurt or cream.

SERVES 6–8

200g (7oz) pitted
   prunes
100ml (3½fl oz) dark rum
Butter or oil, for greasing
75g (2¾oz) wholemeal
   spelt, einkorn or
   wheat flour
2 heaped tbsp cocoa
   powder
75g (2¾oz) light
   muscovado sugar
3 medium eggs
1–2 tsp vanilla extract
500ml (17fl oz) full-fat
   milk or oat milk
100g (3½oz) dark
   chocolate chips

Begin by soaking the prunes in the rum the day before you make the pudding (or warm through in a saucepan and set aside for 30 minutes if you've forgotten).

When ready to cook, preheat the oven to 200°C/180°C fan/gas 6.

Grease a 20–23cm (8–9-inch) ovenproof flan dish with butter or oil and spoon in the prunes (leaving behind any excess rum for your next batch). Place the dish on a large baking tray and heat through in the oven for about 10 minutes.

Put the flour, cocoa powder, sugar, eggs and vanilla extract into a large bowl and use a fork to mix together to a thick paste. Slowly pour in the milk, stirring constantly, until you have a smooth batter.

Remove the dish from the oven, sprinkle the chocolate chips over the prunes and carefully ladle in the batter. Bake in the oven for 30–35 minutes until slightly puffed and a knife comes out clean from the centre.

Leave to rest for at least 15 minutes before eating warm or at room temperature.

TRY THIS
- Make a plain batter without the cocoa and chocolate.
- Macerate halved plums, greengages, mirabelles, apricots or pitted cherries with a few tablespoons of muscovado sugar (and a splash of alcohol such as kirsch, if you like) for 1–2 hours. Arrange in your dish instead of the prunes and continue as above.

Spring

IN SEASON

Artichokes, Asparagus, Broad Beans, Carrots, Chicory,
Cucumbers, Elderflowers, Lettuce, Morel Mushrooms,
New Potatoes, Purple-sprouting Broccoli, Radishes, Rhubarb,
Rocket, Leeks, Samphire, Spinach, Spring Greens,
Spring Onions, Watercress, Wild Garlic

Foraging

Spring is the perfect time to head out into the woods, or to scour the hedgerows, for edible shoots and leaves. It's so easy to forget that collecting wild, seasonal food is how we humans survived for millennia – first as hunter-gatherers, and then more recently as subsistence farmers when foraged foods supplemented our diets.

Nowadays, with fully stocked supermarket shelves throughout the year, we barely notice 'the hungry gap' (that lull in local British produce, from April through to early June), when we rely heavily upon imported food. The lush, wild greens and flowers must have been such a relief in the old days, when our winter vegetables were on their last legs, larders were almost bare and the spring crops were not yet ready for harvest.

While foraging is no longer a matter of necessity for most of us, there's something so gratifying about collecting food for free. Searching for particular leaves, flowers or, later in the season, fruit and berries gives a walk a real purpose; children, in particular, love to have a quest while taking a stroll. Whether focusing on a wild patch in the local park, or searching the length of a rural footpath, being outside and connecting with nature is incredibly positive for all of us.

There are few general rules to keep in mind.

- If in doubt, don't eat it! While some natural harvests are easy to recognise, others require some expertise; thankfully there are plenty of specialist books, online resources and courses on offer to help you on your way. Always use multiple reliable identification guides to be sure about what you are picking and eating, and be aware that some plants have inedible and sometimes poisonous lookalikes.

- Keep to public rights of way and don't trespass on private property without the landowner's permission. A lot of other land is open access for recreation in the UK, but this may not include the right to forage. Do check and follow any rules or signage, particularly on land owned by the National Trust, Forestry Commission or Woodland Trust, as this could be a conservation area or prime habitat. It's best not to forage on Sites of Special Scientific Interest (SSSIs) – ASSIs in Northern Ireland – or National Nature Reserves (NNRs), as they are likely to have bylaws preventing the picking of plants.

- Pick in areas of abundance and take only what you need, leaving behind plenty of leaves, flowers or fruit for wildlife to live on. Over-picking can damage plants and impact the next year's growth. Research thoroughly and collect carefully and selectively. Never pull up plants by the roots.

- Take proper tools like a sharp knife, scissors, garden pruners or secateurs and just cut off leaves, berries and flowers (and stems if using herbs). This will cause less damage to the plants, giving them the best chance to regrow or fruit well the following year.

- Avoid foraging on busy roadsides and water sources, or anywhere dogs are likely to spray, as your bounty may be polluted.

Once you start foraging it can be addictive. Later in the year there are elderberries for tangy sauces, crab apples for jelly, blackberries for crumbles and sloes for gin, as well as a plethora of lesser-known treasures. Further down the line you may well become enchanted by gathering seaweed on our rugged coastline. There really can't be a more pleasurable way of slowing down, reconnecting with the natural world and reliving the ways of our ancient ancestors.

Minimise trampling through undergrowth to get to something else, leave no trace behind, and take care of habitats and the wildlife within them.

Three Spring Favourites to Get you Started

NETTLES
Pick just the top four sets of leaves from young nettles, before they begin to flower (rubber gloves advised).

Once home, give the nettles a rinse and then boil for 2 minutes to remove the sting.

For soup Squeeze excess moisture from the leaves before chopping and adding to a simple potato-based soup for the last 5 minutes of cooking.

For tea Switch off the heat and let the leaves steep for about 10 minutes in the pan, strain, then serve your tea with a little honey, if you like (this is also lovely with a tiny splash of elderflower cordial; see right).

Nettle tea is said to be helpful in treating hay fever, controlling blood sugar, flushing harmful bacteria from the urinary tract, reducing arthritis pain, managing inflammation – it happens to taste pretty good too... so what's not to like?

WILD GARLIC OR RAMSONS
Growing in ancient woodlands, you'll probably catch a waft of wild garlic before you see it. The luscious, shiny leaves will smell intensely garlicky when you crush them in your fingers. The poisonous leaves of Lily of the Valley, and of Lords and Ladies, look similar but will not have the pungent, garlicky odour, so always rip the leaf and sniff. If you're in any doubt about which plant it is, do not eat it.

Wild garlic is perfect for pesto, ripping a little into salads, adding to omelettes, flatbreads or making a chimichurri (page 93). The tiny, six-petalled, star-like flowers are edible too, with an intense burst of garlicky goodness; they look stunning sprinkled over a salad or an open sandwich.

ELDERFLOWERS
Frothy white elderflowers are one of the welcome signs that summer is not far away. Pick the flower heads in the morning, give them a gentle shake to remove any insects and carry home in a basket or loose canvas bag.

MAKES 2 X 750ML (1¼ PINT) BOTTLES

For cordial

- Collect about 20 flower heads.

- Pour 1 litre (1¾ pints) boiling water into a large saucepan, add 1kg (2lb 4oz) caster or granulated sugar and stir to dissolve.

- Add the flowers to the pan with the pared zest and juice of 3 lemons (adding 60g/2¼oz citric acid at this point will give a sharper taste and extend the shelf life from 1 month in the fridge to 4).

- Cover with a cloth or reusable wrap and leave to steep for 24 hours.

- Strain the liquid through a muslin-lined sieve (you can wash and reuse the cloth again and again) into sterilised bottles (page 49).

- Serve with still or sparkling water, or stir into nettle tea, add to gooseberries as they cook or use to macerate strawberries or make a jelly.

Pesto and Other Herby Sauces

Making pesto, 'pounded' sauce, from the Italian verb *pestare*, is an efficient way of prolonging the life of slightly tired herbs. Traditionally, pesto-making involved crushing herbs together with a mortar and pestle. Nowadays a blender or food processor makes light work of whizzing up these versatile mixes: perfect for pasta, pepping up sandwiches, adding instant depth to salads or adding a spoonful to the top of soups.

Pesto is a great way to embrace 'root-to-fruit' eating: try blitzing the ferny leaves from carrot tops or fennel, using peppery radish leaves or deeply savoury celery or even celeriac tops instead of, or as well as, the herbs.

The cheese element could be any hard, mature cheese, which is also a great way to use up heels of Cheddar, Gruyère or other random leftovers. Nutritional yeast makes a great cheese substitute for a dairy-free pesto.

Any nuts or oily seeds can be used: almonds, walnuts, hazelnuts, pine nuts, cashews, peanuts, pecans, pistachios. It's a satisfying way to use up odd ingredients from the baking cupboard, but do test before using, as stale nuts can taste rancid. Roasting will bring out the nutty flavour while raw nuts add a creamy richness.

Pesto alla Genovese is hard to beat, especially when freshly made.

PESTO

Pesto will keep for up to five days in a jar in the fridge. Just cover the pesto with a thin layer of oil to stop it oxidising.

While their high fat content means that pestos aren't ideal for long-term freezing, they will retain their vibrant flavour in the freezer perfectly well for up to six weeks. Flatten the pesto out in a thin layer in a reusable plastic bag; then, when it has frozen like a thin slate, you can just snap off as much of the sauce as you want.

MAKES 1 X 250ML (9FL OZ) JAR

- ½–1 garlic clove, roughly chopped
- 1 large bunch of basil, including roughly chopped tender stalks
- A handful of pine nuts, lightly toasted if you like a nuttier, rather than creamier, pesto
- A handful of grated Parmesan cheese
- 100ml (3½fl oz) extra-virgin olive oil
- Squeeze of fresh lemon juice (optional)
- Salt and pepper (optional)

Blend all the ingredients together to a slightly chunky, textured paste. You're looking for that perfect balance of pungent garlic, aromatic herb, creamy nut or seed, tangy/savoury cheese and rich, characterful oil. Add seasoning if necessary.

Try this:
That's your blueprint – now play around with...

Wild garlic + hulled hemp seeds + extra-virgin olive oil + grated lemon zest and juice + Parmesan.

Garlic + parsley + dill + roasted almonds + extra-virgin olive oil + pecorino.

Garlic + coriander + fresh green chilli + roasted sunflower seeds + rapeseed oil + grated lime zest and juice + nutritional yeast.

ARGENTINIAN CHIMICHURRI

Argentinian Chimichurri is a lighter, zingier option for using fresh herbs and vegetable tops. Here's a classic recipe but feel free to replace some, or all, of the parsley with other herbs, or vegetable tops – wild garlic works wonderfully well.

Chimichurri can be kept in a jar in the fridge for up to a week; just top the sauce with a thin layer of oil to stop it oxidising.

MAKES 1 X 250ML (9FL OZ) JAR

- 1 very large bunch of flat-leaf parsley
- 2 tsp fresh or dried oregano
- 1–2 garlic cloves
- 1–2 fresh red chillies or a pinch of chilli flakes
- 100ml (3½fl oz) extra-virgin olive oil, plus extra for the top
- 2 tbsp red wine, white wine or cider vinegar
- Pinch of salt

Chop the parsley (reserve the parsley stalks for stock), oregano, garlic and chilli very finely. Mix with the olive oil and vinegar, then season with salt and drizzle with oil to serve.

For wild garlic chimichurri, replace half of the parsley with about 10 wild garlic leaves and leave out the garlic cloves.

Warm Lentil Salad with Roasted Radish, Whipped Cheese and Wild Garlic Chimichurri

Ravishing pink radishes burst onto the scene in the spring, shouting for a starring role in refreshing salads, but our British weather can still be a bit dodgy, so it's great to have a warm version up your sleeve. Do try to seek out some wild garlic – a perfect excuse for a walk in the woods – but, failing that, a classic parsley-based chimichurri is a great option too.

SERVES 4

300g (10½oz) small green lentils
1 bay leaf
1 tbsp cider vinegar
3 tbsp olive oil
½ tbsp Dijon mustard
2 bunches of radishes (about 24 radishes)
1 tbsp runny honey or maple syrup
1 quantity Wild Garlic Chimichurri (page 93)
2 tbsp Greek-style yogurt
100g (3½oz) feta
1 tbsp extra-virgin olive oil
Salt and pepper

Place the lentils in a large saucepan with the bay leaf and cover with cold water by about 5cm (2 inches). Bring to the boil, then reduce the heat and simmer for 20–30 minutes until the lentils are tender but still intact. Once cooked, drain the lentils, tip into a large bowl and while still warm, add the vinegar, 2 tbsp of the olive oil and the mustard. Season well with salt and pepper.

Meanwhile, preheat the oven to 220°C/200°C fan/gas 7.

Trim the radishes (reserving their leaves for the chimichurri), cut them in half and tumble them with the honey, the remaining 1 tbsp olive oil and a pinch of salt on a roasting tray. Roast for 15–20 minutes until lightly browned.

Finely chop a handful of the reserved radish leaves and add to the chimichurri.

Beat the yogurt, feta and extra-virgin olive oil together in a bowl with a hand-held blender or a fork.

Tip the hot radishes over the bowl of lentils and serve with separate bowls of the whipped feta and chimichurri alongside.

TRY THIS

The basic lentil salad is worth doubling and keeping in the fridge to bolster other meals during the week. Try serving with piles of ripe tomatoes, slices of fresh peach and a basil dressing in the summer or simply adding the lentils to a vegetable soup to give it more body.

Do play around with this lentil/vegetable/dressing/cheese combination.
- In early summer you can swap in baby turnips and new-season carrots, while slices of squash are a great autumnal option.
- You can revert to a classic parsley-based chimichurri if you can't track down any wild garlic. Any kind of pesto could work well too.
- Try soured cream whipped with blue cheese.

A Monthly Roast

Gathering around the family table on a Sunday, with a joint of meat, or a bird, as the centrepiece, has been a national tradition for centuries. This weekly ritual may be on the wane, but a roast is still the way most of us celebrate Christmas and birthdays, and how we entertain relatives of all ages, or welcome our home leavers back to the nest. A home-cooked roast is like a familiar, loving hug, but how can we make it more sustainable?

Weekly, all-you-can-eat platters of succulent rare beef, or an entire chicken for four, are as costly to you as they are to the planet (page 76), so it makes sense to cut back.

Now, this may sound obvious, but perhaps your roast could become **a monthly ritual**, timed to coincide with a great supplier coming to the local market, or with a visit to a farm shop. It could be the week that the monthly meat box arrives (it's also a good way to keep tabs on how much meat you're consuming and to source directly from ethical producers). The anticipation will make your meal even more of a treat and that high-quality meat will be worth the wait.

There are plenty of ways to lighten your 'food print' when it comes to a classic roast, the most obvious being to **reduce the portions of meat**, but how do you do that without starting a rebellion?

Historically, Yorkshire pudding was served before the more costly meat, to put a dent in everyone's appetite. This sounds counterintuitive after years of being told 'don't snack now, it'll spoil your lunch', but if you have a house full of ravenous teenagers, it could be worth serving something simple and nutritious before lunch. There's the added benefit that you won't have them drooling expectantly over your shoulder as you finish making the gravy. You could serve a bowl of hummus (page 40) with flatbreads (page 128) and chopped vegetables.

Crowd out the meat. Plating the meat yourself keeps control of portion sizes, and then you can have a vast array of vegetables on the table alongside stuffing balls (page 99) or Yorkshire puddings and generous quantities of gravy (whatever you do, don't skimp on the gravy).

Roast vegetables are crowd-pleasers so why not add celeriac, Jerusalem artichokes, carrots, fennel, beetroot or cauliflower to the potatoes and parsnips?

Purées (page 63) can be made ahead of time and reheated just before serving.

Steam-fried Greens (page 73) can be ready to go in the pan.

Yorkshire pudding and stuffing are not only good to eat, but the carbs will fill people up.

Good gravy, or another deeply savoury sauce, is key to a successful low-meat lunch, delivering umami flavour across the plate.

Leftover vegetables are a boon. It's worth increasing the quantities you prepare, just so that you have enough for Bubble and Squeak the following day (page 100).

Enjoy every last scrap of your meat, sliced or shredded for sandwiches, added to an enchilada (page 157), scattered over a salad or grain dish, finely chopped into a ragu (page 158) or thrown into a noodle soup (page 103).

You could also ring the changes with a veggie roast. We're not talking processed faux meat cutlets, and the days of the nut roast are probably gone (a shame, as some recipes are fabulous). How about something that's as delicious as it is dramatic to carve at the table? There are plenty of options such as crispy-glazed cauliflower, celeriac or small squash (page 160).

Roast Chicken

When it comes to a roast that can you can enjoy for most of the week, chicken must surely win the prize. A creative cook can stretch one bird over three to four meals, meaning that the investment in a well-reared fowl pays off. How about Bubble and Squeak (page 100) or Asian Chicken Noodle Soup (page 103)?

Roasting the bird on a bed of vegetables not only guarantees wonderful pan juices for the best gravy ever, but those vegetables can be incorporated into dishes. Don't forget to save your carcass to make a fabulously versatile stock (page 102).

**SERVES 4 +
AT LEAST 8
LEFTOVER
PORTIONS**

1 large onion, quartered
2 celery sticks, halved lengthways
2 carrots, halved lengthways
200ml (7fl oz) water
1 x 1.5–2kg (3¼–4½lb) free-range chicken
1 lemon, quartered
A few sprigs of rosemary, thyme or tarragon
2 tbsp olive oil or soft butter
Giblets, neck and heart (reserving the liver for another dish)
Salt and pepper

Preheat the oven to 200°C/180°C fan/gas 6. Estimate about 35–45 minutes roasting time per 1kg (2lb 4oz), plus 15 minutes to rest.

Place the onion, celery and carrots in a roasting tin with the water.

Stuff the chicken with the lemon and herbs, rub the skin all over with oil or butter and season with salt and pepper. Lay the chicken on its side on top of the vegetables and roast in the middle of the oven.

After 20 minutes turn the chicken over onto the other side, baste with the pan juices (adding a splash of water if it's drying out) and return to the oven for another 20 minutes.

Now turn the chicken upright, adding the giblets (just the neck and heart) to the vegetables and juices under the bird and roast for another 20 minutes.

After a total of 1 hour, test the thickest part of the leg with a skewer – if the juices are clear when the skewer is inserted and the leg joint feels loose and wobbly then your chicken is ready; otherwise return to the oven and roast for another 15–20 minutes until your bird is cooked.

Tip the juices from inside the cavity over the veggies in the roasting tin and set the chicken aside to rest on a warmed platter, covered with foil. Serve with gravy.

TRY THIS SIMPLE GRAVY

Add a couple of spoonfuls of the fatty juices from the roasting tin to a saucepan and stir in 1 heaped tbsp of plain flour. Cook over a medium heat until the flour begins to swell and thicken. Now strain the vegetables and giblets (if you had some) from the roasting tin, slowly adding their liquid to the gravy, stirring constantly to avoid lumps. Top up the gravy with a splash of white wine, cooking liquid from any vegetable or even some water along with 1 tsp Marmite, then season to taste.

Reserve the strained vegetables (removing the giblets) from under the bird for tomorrow's Bubble and Squeak (page 100).

Stuffing Balls

Brilliant for adding more textures and flavours to any roast – and filling, for those with voracious appetites. Once you have the knack you can throw these together with all manner of extra ingredients, such as nuts, seeds, dried apricots, sun-dried tomatoes, dried mushrooms or some grated cheese.

MAKES 8

30g (1oz or 2 tbsp) butter, rapeseed oil or olive oil, plus extra oil for drizzling
1 medium onion, diced
1 celery stick, diced
100g (3½oz) coarse, fresh breadcrumbs made from stale bread
1 small apple (cooker or eater), grated, peel and all
A handful of herbs, such as thyme, sage, parsley or rosemary, very finely chopped
Finely grated zest of ½ lemon
1 tbsp ground chia, flax- or camelina seeds mixed with 3 tbsp water or 1 egg, beaten
Extra-virgin olive oil, for drizzling
Salt and pepper

Heat the butter or oil in a frying pan over a medium heat and fry the onion and the celery for 8–10 minutes until soft.

Mix the breadcrumbs, apple, herbs, lemon zest and the sticky seed mixture together in a large bowl. Add the onion, celery and any oil from the pan and stir to combine, then season with salt and pepper to taste.

Mould the mixture into 8 even-sized balls, squeezing firmly so that they hold together.

Place the balls on a baking tray, drizzle with extra oil and roast until crisped and golden, for about 20–30 minutes at about 180–200°C/160–180°C fan/gas 4–6 (they are pretty forgiving, so can just fit in with your other oven temperatures for the rest of the roast).

TIP
Camelina seed, also known as Gold of Pleasure, has been grown in Britain for centuries. The seeds are loaded with omega-3 fatty acids and are perfect used instead of flax seeds or chia seeds in baked goods, for sprinkling and also, owing to their mucilaginous qualities, for thickening smoothies or replacing eggs in vegan baking (see Resources on page 184 for some suppliers).

Bubble and Squeak

Homemade bubble and squeak is a million miles from anything you might get on a pub menu. It's about the brilliance of leftovers, building on all the fabulous flavours of the previous meal; it's worth cooking extra vegetables whenever you prepare a roast.

The potatoes and greens are essential, but you might have leftover carrots or roasted parsnips too, if you've roasted your poultry on top of some vegetables (see Roast Chicken, page 98). Adding these will be the icing on the cake.

SERVES 4

3 tbsp olive oil
1 onion, sliced
500g (1lb 2oz) leftover mashed, boiled or roast potatoes (or any mix of these, roughly chopped)
300g (10½oz) finely shredded kale, Brussels sprouts, spring greens, cabbage or chard, plus any leftover vegetables from your roast)
Pinch of salt
2–3 tbsp Worcestershire sauce (there are vegan versions too)
Simple Ruby Sauerkraut (see page 48), to serve

Heat the olive oil in a large frying pan over a low heat and fry the onion for 10 minutes. You want to soften and sweeten the onion rather than brown it.

Once the onion is translucent, add the potatoes, greens, any other leftover vegetables and a good pinch of salt. Increase the heat to high and fry, stirring occasionally, until the vegetables brown and begin to catch on the pan as they cook. If your vegetables do stubbornly stick to the base of the pan just remove it from the heat and wait for a minute. The moisture in the vegetables will help to steam and loosen everything.

Now scrape the bottom of the pan with a flat-ended wooden spoon to loosen the crusty bits, stir and return to the heat to repeat the process; caramelisation is the key to a really good bubble and squeak.

When the greens have fully wilted and you have plenty of crusty browned potato, add half the Worcestershire sauce. Stir through well, then taste, adding more sauce as required. Serve with sauerkraut.

TRY THIS
- A little leftover gravy can be added instead of the Worcestershire sauce, should you happen to have some.
- Top your Bubble and Squeak with a fried or poached egg and perhaps a thin slice of chicken, plus a zingy pickle or chutney, and you have a plate to rival, or often better, the roast you started with.

Stock: A Kitchen Basic

Homemade stock is a no-brainer. Sustainable cooking has to be pocket- as well as planet-friendly; traditional stocks are about as frugal as it gets, made from vegetable scraps and leftover bones. A good stock adds essential depth to dishes such as risotto or speltotto (page 82), to stews, soups and sauces; served as a broth, stock plays centre stage in one of the most restorative of dishes.

Get into the habit of setting aside those tough outer layers of onion from just below the skin, carrot peelings (scrub the carrots before peeling to get rid of any grit), stringy outer sticks of celery and parsley stalks. You won't always have time to make stock immediately, so you can have an ongoing trimmings bag that lives in the freezer. The day you feel like making a simple vegetable stock, or have some leftover chicken, fish or beef bones, you'll be ready to go.

VEGETABLE STOCK
Makes about 1 litre (1¾ pints)
Add about 200g (7oz) each onion, carrot and celery, a few parsley stalks, roughly chopped, 1 bay leaf and 6 black peppercorns to a large saucepan and cover with cold water. Simmer for about 1 hour. Strain, cool, then store in the fridge for up to 4 days or freezer for up to 6 months.

POULTRY STOCK –
CHICKEN, TURKEY, GUINEA FOWL
Makes about 1 litre (1¾ pints)
The perfect way to make the most of a chicken carcass – raw or once you've stripped away the roasted meat. No carcass? Six chicken wings will give great flavour. Add your bones or wings and the vegetable stock ingredients, along with 3 tbsp white wine or white wine vinegar, to a large saucepan. Cover with cold water and simmer for 3–6 hours for a rich stock. Strain, cool quickly, then store in the fridge for up to 4 days or freezer for up to 6 months.

BEEF STOCK
Makes about 1 litre (1¾ pints)
You may be able to persuade your butcher or meat supplier to sell, or give you, some bones, or you might have some from a joint. Preheat the oven to 200°C/180°C fan/gas 6 and roast the bones for 45 minutes before adding to the vegetable stock ingredients. Simmer for 6–12 hours for an intense beefy broth. Strain, cool quickly, then store in the fridge for up to 4 days or freezer for up to 6 months.

FISH STOCK
Makes about 1 litre (1¾ pints)
This can be the base of a great soup or stew. Use the bones of white fish, as oily fish such as tuna and mackerel make a greasy, pungent stock. Prawn shells and heads make superb stock. Wash the bones thoroughly. Add the bones, skin and fish heads to the vegetable stock ingredients, along with 2 slices of lemon. Bring to a simmer and cook for 30 minutes. Strain, cool quickly, then store in the fridge for up to 4 days or freezer for up to 6 months.

General Tips
For a perfect, clear stock, skim off any foam that rises to the top as the pan comes to a simmer, and avoid boiling. Fat can be skimmed off the surface as the stock cools.

Make stocks in large quantities, and then, once strained, boil to reduce down. Freeze in yogurt pots, jars or reused freezer bags.

It's worth considering the source of heat you are using when cooking beef and poultry stocks. A slow cooker or crockpot is an economical way (start on high for 1 hour, then reduce to low for the remaining time). Pressure cookers speed up the entire process and give an equally nutritious and deeply savoury result.

Three Ways with Homemade Chicken Stock

ASIAN CHICKEN NOODLE SOUP

SERVES 4

Bring 1.5 litres (2½ pints) chicken stock, 2 tsp grated fresh root ginger, 1 crushed garlic clove and 2 finely sliced lemongrass sticks to the boil in a large saucepan.

Once boiling, add 120–150g (4–5oz) noodles (the choice is yours, but soba noodles, which contain a proportion of buckwheat, are particularly satisfying) and 200g (7oz) any finely sliced vegetable, such as carrots, courgette, broccoli or peppers.

Boil until the noodles are tender, then season with soy sauce and lime juice. Sprinkle over 4 finely sliced spring onions, a handful of coriander or basil leaves and 1–2 finely chopped red or green chillies. Serve.

ITALIAN-STYLE BRODO

SERVES 4

Bring 1.5 litres (2½ pints) chicken stock, and an old Parmesan rind, if you have one, to enrich the soup, to the boil in a large saucepan.

Add a few handfuls of tiny pasta such as the diminutive stars or alphabet shapes (or snap up a few bits of spaghetti into tiny pieces) and cook for about 5 minutes, or until the pasta is tender.

Season with salt and pepper and serve with grated Parmesan.

FREESTYLE

SERVES 4

Bring 1.5 litres (2½ pints) stock to the boil in a large saucepan. Add about 2–3 ladlefuls of any variety of cooked pulse or wholegrain that takes your fancy, then stir in some chopped greens for the last minute or two.

Season, then top with pesto, a squeeze of lemon juice and maybe a few strips of cooked chicken if you have some left over from a roast.

Celebration Spring Salad

In late spring the greengrocer's shelves are loaded with local goodies: bunches of radishes and asparagus, paper sacks of new potatoes and even the early pods of peas and broad beans. It's time to celebrate the first produce of the year. Serving this salad while the potatoes are still warm intensifies all the flavours.

SERVES 4 AS A MAIN COURSE SALAD

600g (1lb 5oz) new potatoes, halved if larger than bite-sized
1 sprig of mint
100ml (3½fl oz) extra-virgin olive oil
300g (10½oz) asparagus spears
200g (7oz) baby broad beans
75g (2¾oz) pea shoots, washed
12 radishes, quartered (soaking the radishes in ice-cold water for 20 minutes before chopping will give crisp results)
Salt

Dressing
Juice of 1 lemon
3 tbsp crème fraîche or soured cream (oat-based crème fraîche is a dairy-free option)
1 tsp Dijon mustard
1 small bunch of chives, finely chopped with scissors
Pinch of salt and plenty of pepper

Optional
A few crispy bacon lardons, or some cooked chicken, or flakes of cooked salmon (150g/5oz portion of fillet), or halved soft-boiled eggs, or a handful of roasted almonds

Boil the potatoes and mint in a large saucepan of salted water for 15 minutes, or until tender, then drain and return to the pan, discarding the mint sprig. Toss with half of the olive oil, then cover with the lid and set aside to keep warm.

Meanwhile, prepare the asparagus. Remove any woody tips (save those for stock, page 102), chop off about 5cm (2 inches) of the stalk ready for steaming or boiling, and sliver the top of the spears into ribbons using a potato peeler. Set aside.

If you have a steamer pan, steam the asparagus stalks over the potatoes for 5 minutes, or until tender; otherwise, cook them in a saucepan of boiling water for about 3 minutes. Drain and plunge into a large bowl of cold water to refresh and keep their colour.

Steam or blanch the broad beans for 3–5 minutes until just tender, then drain and pop them from their skins.

Mix all the dressing ingredients together in a bowl along with the remaining olive oil. Pour the dressing into a large salad bowl, add most of the pea shoots, the radishes, cooked asparagus, asparagus ribbons, broad beans and warm potatoes (keeping a few of each ingredient back to garnish the bowl), then turn everything together, taking care not to break up the potatoes. Sprinkle over the reserved vegetables and any of the optional toppings and serve while warm.

Food Recycling

However careful you are with your fridge and larder management there will inevitably be some food waste. You'll find some tips in the Root to Fruit section (page 70) on how to minimise this, but there are only so many onion skins that can end up in a stock.

Food waste is a relatively new phenomenon; historically, food scraps would be fed to the household pig or the chickens or otherwise end up on the compost heap to be spread back onto the land. Nowadays, a tiny percentage of us keep livestock and, even if we do, there are strict regulations when it comes to feeding them scraps. The one option that is open to most of us, and should be open to all, is composting or food recycling.

Composting is a vital, and often overlooked, cog in the wheel of life, converting our rubbish into valuable feed or humus (and that has nothing to do with mezze) for our soil, as well as reducing greenhouse gas emissions. In a nutshell, the food waste that is buried in tons of household waste in regular landfills will decompose under anaerobic conditions, producing vast quantities of methane. Meanwhile, smaller-scale composting is aerated by intermittent turning over of the waste, during which, instead of producing methane, the microbes use carbon for energy and lock the remaining carbon in the soil as humus (the rich, dark, decayed matter produced at the end of composting).

You can compost pretty much all food other than meat, fish and dairy, which decompose very slowly, can create an unpleasant smell and could attract rats and other pests. Even basic cardboard can be ripped up and composted, but not the waxed or lined types such as takeaway drink cups. In fact, a composting system is all about a balance (of a ratio of 2:3) of the nitrogen-rich green waste (vegetable scraps, grass clippings, coffee grounds) to the carbon-rich brown waste (cardboard, newspaper, sawdust, dry leaves, branches and twigs).

Home Composting Options

While you can find entire tomes on composting, or watch passionate gardeners giving endless tutorials online, it's sometimes good to get back to basics and talk through the options, so here are most of them.

If you are lucky enough to have a garden, or an allotment, then a compost heap or trench is probably already part of your life. If it's not, what's stopping you? A successful compost heap requires a space about 91cm (3ft) square, and should be no deeper than 1.5m (5ft), otherwise the pressure of the weight of your compost will push out the air that's needed for decomposition. It's a question of turning over the compost every other week and checking that it is fairly moist, and then a few months of waiting.

If you have a small garden then **compact compost bins** are readily available (or you could fashion your own from an old rubbish bin with a few strategically placed draining holes). Here, rather than turning the compost in a traditional way with a garden fork, you aerate the bin with a pole called an aerator, a bit like a corkscrew, or a stick with a barb. Most bins have a small door at the bottom from which to access your compost. **Tumbling composters**, that look, and work, rather like a giant tombola drum, save you the trouble of turning your compost but do require some space.

A **wormery** could be an option if you're stuck for space, as it can live on a balcony or inside the house. While some people might feel squeamish about the thought of a bin filled with Tiger worms working their way through the kitchen waste, children often love the idea, and it is a valuable lesson in the cycle of nature. Not only will you get a ready supply of rich liquid fertiliser, often known as worm tea, but also the bonus that vermicomposting is one of the quickest methods – so you won't have to wait too long for it to be ready. Downsides are perhaps a smaller capacity than a classic compost bin and the fact that you have to be careful about what you recycle (the worms don't appreciate too much acidity).

Another indoor possibility is a Japanese **Bokashi bin** where you can place all your food waste (including meat and fish) in a tub layered with Bokashi bran that's loaded with bacteria which will ferment your scraps. You will be able to drain off a liquid fertiliser, but your solid waste will require further composting in a hole in the garden or on your conventional compost heap. The great advantage is that you can have usable compost in a little over a month, whereas conventional compost will usually take at least six months and regular turning to reach the same stage.

Electric **countertop 'composters' and food recyclers** are worth researching, although they can be pricey and require a small amount of energy to run. Some versions grind and dehydrate the food while others involve microbial action. The product is a soil improver rather than compost, but certainly a valid option that beats sending food to landfill.

Municipal or large-scale food recycling
Many councils have a regular kerbside food recycling collection service, and, if yours doesn't, then it's time to get lobbying. For the many of us who lack the space, time, or perhaps the inclination to compost at home, kerbside food recycling is the solution to keeping food waste out of landfill.

Your waste may be composted along with garden waste in a closed system for up to a month at temperatures of up to 70°C (158°F), speeding up the decomposition and killing off any potentially harmful microbes. The waste is then matured for a few months outside and used as a soil improver.

Alternatively, the food may be broken down by anaerobic digestion in an enclosed system, giving off methane, just as it would be in a landfill situation, but the gas is collected and converted into biogas and used to create fuel or heat or to generate electricity. The broken-down waste can then be used as fertiliser.

Food Recycling is an Absolute No-brainer:
- **We can reduce food waste going into landfill sites** and, in turn, reduce greenhouse gas emissions.

- **We can save money, reducing the need for commercial composts** – many of which contain peat, which is a massive problem.

- **We can reconnect with the cycle of life**, giving back to the earth.

Get Growing

However big or small your space, growing food from scratch is one of the most rewarding things to do.

Healthwise, gardening isn't just about keeping fit; it's also about mental well-being. If you do have access to some space outside, breathing the fresh air, and focusing away from work or day-to-day stresses, can be amazingly therapeutic. Many doctors are prescribing gardening nowadays to help beat anxiety and depression.

Growing food reconnects us with nature, and, particularly for kids, is a way of tracking food, quite literally, back to its roots. We're so much more appreciative of food, and less likely to waste it, when we understand how it's produced.

You will have super-fresh produce on your doorstep that can be picked literally minutes before you dive in, retaining its full flavour and nutrient potential. Is there anything better than a fully ripened tomato, straight from the vine?

Homegrown food can be cost effective too. Even if you're only talking about half a dozen pots of herbs on the windowsill, you can save money. You're cutting out the transportation and unnecessary packaging as well.

From a conservation perspective, many of us could do with greening up our outdoor spaces. Insect numbers are in catastrophic decline, including the pollinators that are absolutely fundamental to the health of the environment. City gardens are often virtually devoid of life, crammed with decking, gravel, patio slabs and, increasingly, metre upon metre of Astroturf. Everything focuses on easy maintenance, ignoring the fact that nurturing plants and watching wildlife can be a wonderful hobby rather than a chore. Growing food in harmony with nature in our own backyard is a very positive step.

One Step At a Time

If starting to grow your own fruit and vegetables at home feels too daunting a prospect, how about joining a community project? There are more and more social farms and community gardens springing up around the country, offering a chance to learn from experts, to bring more biodiversity into the neighbourhood and to share in the joy of producing food.

We can all start small at home, making the most of the space we have, planting up a window box or packing a balcony with pots. Herbs, such as mint, parsley and basil, are a great starting point.

Salad leaves are another option, as they shoot so quickly and many can be grown as a cut-and-come-again crop, where you regularly cut a few leaves from each plant and more regrow. Choosing leaves with a distinctive punch, such as rocket, sorrel, mizuna and mustard, means that you can easily pep up a simple head of bought lettuce or a few spinach leaves. If, on the other hand, you're trying to encourage children to enjoy salads (which can be quite a challenge), there's no better place to start than growing some pea shoots.

Grow Your Own Pea Shoots

Growing a few shoots on the windowsill is a great option for novice gardeners; they will be ready to eat in a couple of weeks and there's no danger of marauding slugs.

The delicate nutty flavour, just like a leafy version of a sweet fresh pea, along with the pretty twining tendrils of pea shoots make them a fabulous addition to any salad. Kids who dislike lettuce are much more likely to dive into something with a familiar flavour that they've nurtured and harvested themselves.

You will need:
- Dried peas (rather than seeds, just buy the cooking ingredients)
- Seed trays or recycled plastic food trays, about 6–10cm (2½–4 inches) deep
- Peat-free, multipurpose potting compost (which is lighter than garden compost)

Soak the peas in cold water overnight.

Check that your container has some small holes in the bottom if you are recycling a plastic food tray. Fill the tray with compost until it's 2cm (¾ inch) from the top, breaking up any lumps in your fingers as you go. Press it down lightly to create an even surface and water well.

Spread over a layer of peas, about 1cm (½ inch) apart. Sprinkle over a layer of compost to completely cover the peas, then water gently using a rose on the watering can.

Place the trays on a sunny windowsill and keep the compost moist, watering every 1–2 days depending on the weather.

In a couple of weeks, once your pea shoots are about 10cm (4 inches) tall, you can harvest them. Snip or pinch the stalk just above the bottom pair of leaves so that your pea shoot can regrow for a second or, if you're lucky, third harvest.

Pea shoots are fabulous added to sandwiches and make a tasty garnish for soups, dips, burgers and fritters. Other microgreens like red mustard, rocket and fennel are also easy to grow.

Tip
No watering can with a rose? You can make your own watering bottle by poking plenty of small holes in the lid of a plastic milk bottle using a hammer and nail.

No Room For a Veg Patch?

If you already have a vegetable patch or allotment, you'll have experienced the delight and pride in growing food to share at the table. Many of us have smaller spaces, or in many cases the back garden is primarily a place to relax and enjoy the flowers – and yet gardens can be both beautiful and productive, with a mixture of ornamental plants, fruit and vegetables.

You don't have to dig up your lawn or turn the entire flower bed into a vegetable patch; there are so many edible plants that are also stunning to look at. In a French, *potager*-style garden, flowers are not just there to look pretty but are grown as companion plants to the vegetables, to attract pollinators and to detract, or even divert, pests as well. Many of these companion plants have the added bonus that their leaves or flowers are edible.

Here are just a few edible, flowering companion plants that you might like to grow:

Marigolds, with their fabulous golds and oranges, not only add a huge pop of colour to the garden, but the petals can be sprinkled over salads, into rice or scattered on cupcakes. The blooms attract pollinators such as bees, predators such as ladybirds and hoverflies (which feed on pests such as aphids, whitefly and mites) and they're great for attracting butterflies.

Nasturtiums are easy to grow and look beautiful climbing and tumbling around the garden. The flamboyant flowers and peppery leaves are great in salads and utter perfection in a ham sandwich. As well as being good for pollinators, nasturtiums attract blackfly and cabbage moths that could otherwise be attacking your vegetables (trim away any infected stems or leaves).

Scented geraniums (pelargoniums) are one of the easiest and most rewarding pot, or garden, plants to grow. There are many varieties with delicate flowers that vary in colour from barely pink to fuchsia, while the deeply scented leaves can vary from rose to chocolate and citrus to cola. The leaves can be used to scent jams, teas, custards and bakes. Meanwhile, the plant attracts ladybirds, moths and butterflies.

When it comes to **herbs**, not only will they increase your game in the kitchen, but many are beneficial for insects once they have bolted and are left to flower. The tiny, frothy flowers of coriander, parsley, dill and fennel attract ladybirds and hoverflies whose larvae control aphids and other pests. Basil, rosemary and lemon thyme have often been grown near to windows to repel mosquitos and flies.

You can intersperse the companion plants with tasty, good-looking vegetables such as rainbow chard, purple kale or cavolo nero. Towering globe artichokes and feathery fennel, red and green cabbages... There are so many vivid colours and shapes to play with. Wigwams of peas and runner beans and teepees of squash or cucumbers can be stunning to look at as well as hugely productive. An old bathtub or even a compost sack is perfect for growing potatoes, and a few pots of tomatoes in a sunny spot could bring great rewards in late summer.

Socca with Asparagus and Creamed Cannellini

Socca is a magical thing: it's simply a batter of chickpea flour, salt and water that thickens up and crisps at the edges with nothing but a splash of olive oil and some intense heat. You can use your socca as a base for roasted or grilled vegetables, as a snack cut into triangles with pesto or even instead of a pizza base.

SERVES 4

200g (7oz) chickpea flour (gram flour or besan)
1 tsp salt
400ml (14fl oz) water
3 tbsp extra-virgin olive oil, plus extra to serve
2 bunches of asparagus, trimmed of tough stumps (keep these for a stock later)
Salt and pepper

Creamed cannellini

1 garlic clove, crushed
400g (14oz) can cannellini beans, drained (250g/9oz drained weight)
1 tbsp almond butter, or 1 tbsp ground almonds soaked in 1 tbsp boiling water for 5 minutes
2 tbsp extra-virgin olive oil
2 tbsp lemon juice
2 tbsp grated Parmesan, or 1 tbsp nutritional yeast (for vegan version)

Tip the chickpea flour and salt into a large bowl and slowly whisk in the water and 1 tbsp of the oil until you have a loose, lump-free batter. Cover with a tea towel and leave to rest at room temperature for at least 1 hour, and up to 12: a perfect time to whizz up your creamed cannellini.

For the creamed cannellini, purée all the ingredients together until smooth, then set aside.

Traditional socca is made in flat tins in a very hot oven, but you can save energy making it in a non-stick frying pan. It's easier to make individual socca in a small pan, about 20cm (8 inches) in diameter, if you are planning to flip them overusing a fish slice, but you can use a larger pan and place it under a hot grill to finish (check that the handle is heatproof first!).

Add a dash of oil to your pan, swirling it to create a non-stick surface. Now tip in the batter to a depth of about 1cm (½ inch) and fry over a medium heat for about 5 minutes. Once the socca has set underneath and moves in the pan when you give it a shake (it might require a little bit of help with your fish slice), you can carefully turn it over – this is not a crêpe so it will still be runny on the top. Fry on the other side for 3–4 minutes until golden or place the pan under a hot grill until crisp and set.

Season well with pepper and serve while still warm. You can stack the socca on a warm plate and cover with a saucepan lid to keep warm, if needed.

For the asparagus, bring a pan (big enough for your asparagus) of salted water to the boil and cook the asparagus for 3–5 minutes until tender.

Serve the socca with a couple of spoonfuls of the cannellini cream spread roughly on top (use the back of a spoon). Arrange the asparagus on top and splash with olive oil, a pinch of salt and plenty of pepper.

TIPS

For a local twist, if you can find British pea flour, or fava bean flour, use this instead of the chickpea flour. You can add finely chopped herbs to the batter – rosemary is a classic.

Smaller Plates, Smaller Portions

We all have different appetites; we're different sexes, different heights and builds, with different metabolic rates and a whole host of different lifestyles; there is no one-size-fits-all when it comes to portion size. What is certain, with obesity levels on the rise, is that most of us are eating too much. So, how do we cut back without resorting to unrealistic and unsustainable dieting?

Just look at a 1960s dinner plate: it's about two-thirds of the size of today's. Eating from smaller plates is a great step to being more conscious of just how much we are eating, cutting back without any sense of deprivation or obsessing over calories.

A serving dish in the middle of the table allows everyone to help themselves, with smaller plates automatically controlling the portions. We can always have seconds, but it becomes an active choice, rather than simply eating a huge plate clean without a second thought. Less food will end up in the bin too, as everything left on the serving dish can be turned into tomorrow's leftover creation.

Sales of takeaways and home-delivery restaurant food have rocketed in the last few years and, perhaps in a bid to make customers feel that they're getting value for money, the portion sizes are often quite ludicrous. Getting into the habit of serving food on home crockery makes sense; it's all too easy to mindlessly munch your way through a box of fish and chips that could have fed a family.

Dining out can be another 'eatathon', when it feels embarrassing, or wasteful, not to finish an often-oversized plate of food, and most of us are too embarrassed to ask for a 'doggy bag'. A three-course restaurant meal is a lot of food, so how about choosing two starters or sharing a main course along with a couple of vegetable sides, or perhaps splitting the pudding?

Food on the move is often an overeating trap, where retailers seem to have made meal deals the norm. Why just buy the sandwich that you set out for, if you can get a packet of crisps or a snack, plus a sugary soda thrown in, for next to nothing? If you can get around to it, a homemade sandwich or salad, or a soup whizzed up from last night's leftovers, will be cheaper, healthier and more varied – and you'll be in charge of the portion size. Getting into a routine of forward planning can really make a difference.

Quite obviously, quantity is just one concern when it comes to eating in a healthy way, but if we get used to eating a bit less or being more conscious of how much we are consuming, then perhaps we can put a halt to the nation's ever-expanding waistlines and the epidemic of yo-yo dieting.

For the majority, eating less is a step towards keeping ourselves in good shape, both mentally and physically, but even more important is *what* we eat. Calories have become an obsession. Calories in, calories out. These calculations don't take into account whether you're eating a bowl of dal with brown rice and spinach or a nutritionally bankrupt processed burger in a white bun.

What to Eat Now: More of the Good Stuff

Deciding what to eat has become such a complicated business: there are dieticians, nutritionists, food writers, influencers and even politicians constantly giving advice. Supermarkets are piled with thousands of products: most of them processed, many purporting to be healthy, others extraordinarily convenient and very hard to resist. We're bombarded with advertising and influenced by marketing, some so artful that we're not even aware of it.

We're being told what not to eat and pretty much everything that's highly processed is on that list, but there are moments at the motorway services or train station when it's just about impossible not to eat junk food. If that's a once-in-a-blue-moon scenario then it's not worth losing sleep over, but if it's a regular occurrence then it's time to make a change.

Dieting can be depressing, and even more so when your New Year's resolution to give up biscuits and cakes fails dismally on day five as you're offered a slice of a colleague's birthday cake. A good appetite has to be about balance.

Rather than counting calories, we'd all do much better to increase the ratio of natural, whole foods in our diet. They are more filling and keep you energised for longer – and don't worry; that doesn't mean you need to be fanatical about it. Whole food can be fruit or vegetables, nuts, grains and legumes, and even meat, fish and dairy – just food that hasn't been processed. If you do crowd your shopping basket, your fridge, your cupboards, and ultimately your plate, with loads of good stuff, there isn't much space left for the less nutritious, industrially produced food. That's not to say that you should give up your classic white pasta when you next make spaghetti alla carbonara; just make it less often, and maybe opt for a chickpea and aubergine curry with brown rice the following day.

Our food choices come down to habit and it's usually best to make changes one step at a time, particularly when trying to get other family members on side. Try piling chopped vegetables, such as carrot sticks and slithers of red pepper, with a hummus (pages 40–41) on the table when famished kids come in from school; they'll probably dive in like vultures (you will too), and then there's less hunger for the commercial snacks that are so often packed with calories but virtually devoid of nutrients.

Eating a main course with a variety of fibre-rich wholesome food, that just happens to be delicious, will leave you with less room for dessert. If you do like to eat pudding after every meal then perhaps swap for better choices rather than going cold turkey. Start off with a piece of seasonal fruit on alternate days instead of your sugar fix, or buy natural yogurt rather than super-sweet, flavoured varieties and add a little fruit and honey yourself. Small swaps will ultimately make a difference.

If you have a sweet tooth when it comes to hot drinks, instead of turning to artificial sweeteners (which come with their own health risks), try reducing the sugar in your tea or coffee over a couple of weeks before leaving it out altogether. You'll miss it to begin with, but try your original drink a month later and your palate will have adapted: you'll most likely find it unpleasantly sweet. The same goes with reducing jam on your toast or honey in your porridge. So often you'll find, with time, that less really is more.

Banana, Cardamom and Dark Chocolate Bites

Mini bakes: sweet and truly indulgent in small bite form, reducing the sugar hit, and perfect for feeding a crowd with just one batch of baking. Their diminutive size somehow makes them seem more of an elegant treat than a slice of cake, especially if you can find the oval 'friand' moulds (see tips below), although a mini muffin tin will work very well.

The moisture from both the banana and the almonds stops these little beauties drying out and they will keep for 3–4 days in a tin, or can be frozen and then 'refreshed' for 5 minutes in an oven preheated to 180°C/160°C fan/gas 4 when ready to eat.

MAKES ABOUT 24 MINI FRIANDS, ABOUT 5CM (2 INCHES) X 2CM (¾ INCH) IN DIAMETER OR 12–16 MINI MUFFINS

60g (2¼oz) butter, melted and slightly cooled, or 60ml (4 tbsp) sunflower or rapeseed oil, plus extra for greasing
150g (5oz) ripe bananas, peeled weight (about 2 small bananas)
½ tsp cardamom seeds (you'll need to crush open the pods if you can't buy seeds)
60g (2¼oz) dark chocolate chips, or chopped chocolate from a bar
60g (2¼oz) wholemeal plain flour
1 tsp baking powder
60g (2¼oz) ground almonds
75g (2¾oz) light muscovado sugar
1 large egg

TRY THIS

This is a great way of using up any overripe, brown-speckled bananas languishing in the fruit bowl. If you've no time to bake today you can freeze whole bananas, skin and all.

Silicone friand moulds are now widely available. It may be worth investing in some if you plan to freeze Fruit Purée Bullets (page 154), baby purées (page 40) or concentrated stocks.

Preheat the oven to 200°C/180°C fan/gas 6. Grease a mini muffin tin or friand moulds.

Put the bananas into a large bowl and mash to a rough purée with the back of a fork. Bruise the cardamom seeds in a mortar with a pestle, just enough to crack them but without grinding to a powder (you want intense pops of flavour rather than a homogenous taste). Add the cardamom seeds and the chocolate to the banana and stir.

Sift the wholemeal flour with the baking powder into a separate bowl and stir in the ground almonds.

Put the melted butter (or oil), sugar and egg into a stand mixer fitted with a whisk attachment and whisk at medium speed until frothy and pale (or use hand-held electric beaters in a large bowl, but whisking by hand will take some serious elbow grease). Now fold in the banana mixture and the dry flour ingredients with a large metal spoon. Try not to overmix or you will lose precious air. It may look slightly curdled, but fear not – that's just the texture of the almonds.

Spoon into your prepared moulds, filling to about two-thirds full (put silicone moulds on a baking tray before filling), then bake in the centre of the oven for 15–18 minutes until browned and well risen (mini muffins may take 20 minutes). Leave to cool in the moulds on a wire rack, then pop out and eat warm or at room temperature.

A Young Appetite

Enjoying a nutritious diet is just about the most important thing that our children can do as they grow up – affecting their health, growth, mental development, energy levels and mood. While there's no one-size-fits-all game plan, when it comes to getting kids to eat well there are some good pointers to encourage a 'good appetite'.

Sharing our food together from the earliest age possible, as they do in Mediterranean countries, and in most of the developing world, creates a natural environment in which children see adults relishing good food. Infants constantly copy behaviour as they develop, and so it's no good feeding broccoli to the babes while parents tuck into burger and chips for the fifth night running; we're the role models. Cooking one meal for everyone, as soon as you've passed the baby weaning stage, is less work for you and is much less likely to create fussy eaters.

Our appetite, and love for certain foods, is all about familiarity; if you grow up in India you're surrounded by spices and will, in almost every case, seek out aromatic, fully flavoured dishes for the rest of your life. In the same way, your teenage child is unlikely to welcome a spinach risotto if they've spent the first decade of their life consuming a diet based around sausages and fish fingers.

Familiarity comes not just from eating foods, but from seeing them regularly on the table, handling them and, yes, even playing with them. 'Don't play with your food.' Who doesn't remember being reprimanded thus as a child? Nowadays research has shown that once children have had a chance to get to know a fruit or vegetable, using all their senses in a curious and playful way, they are more inclined to try it. It's hardly surprising that toddlers are hardwired to be suspicious of new foods; for thousands of years that suspicion was crucial to our survival as hunter-gatherers.

Growing food, even just nurturing a pot of basil on the windowsill, helps to close the disconnect between the world outside and what's on our plates. When children pick an apple from a tree or dig up a magical hoard of potatoes, they can begin to appreciate what an incredible gift nature has given to us, and the senseless waste of throwing out something that took so long to grow.

Cooking with children is a fabulous way to create excitement and positive energy around food. You don't have to set aside an afternoon, and there's no need to buy colour-coordinated mini chef outfits or bake bread in twee flowerpots. Cooking with children can be as simple as them spinning the salad dry or sprinkling breadcrumbs on top of a pie. Repetitive tasks, such as shaping fritters or being in charge of the vinaigrette, build confidence. Further down the line, creating an entire dish can be empowering for a kid – especially if that dish is then shared for supper. The pride and joy involved in preparing and sharing good food is addictive and a wonderful way to create a good relationship with food.

Choice is another powerful tool, and we're not talking about the toss-up between a dinosaur-shaped turkey nugget and a homemade courgette and cannellini fritter (we probably know where that would go). Choice can be about a serving platter in the middle of the table, with an assortment of different foods to which everyone helps themselves. Salads, which don't often appeal to kids, can be a great place to start. Lining up strips of different vegetables with some chunks of cheese, nuts, olives and toasted seeds in a rainbow design can encourage experimentation. Give choice; we all love our own bit of independence and freedom. Just make it a choice between all the good stuff.

Our kids may avoid certain foods time and time again when we give them choice, but as long as somebody is eating those foods then you're not wasting anything. Eventually most children will cave in to curiosity, or a desire to appear grown up, and their diets will gradually widen. It's all about the carrot, rather than the stick, approach.

Making the table (yes: that's the table, and not the bedroom desk or sofa) a positive space is important. Once mealtimes become a battleground, or a means of leverage for treats later in the day, children (in particular, toddlers) sense the tension and can begin to use food to push boundaries. Likes, dislikes and, in some cases, all out repulsion around certain foods are natural. It can be about texture or appearance, so it's worth trying different ways of serving the same food. A child who refuses to eat tomatoes may love them in a gazpacho. Forcing a kid to eat a particular food, or punishing them for not doing so, will only reinforce their negative feelings about it; you're always better to focus on the positive.

Children are often ravenous when they get home from school, so this is the time to have plenty of tasty, healthy snack options to hand: hummus and other dips, plenty of fresh vegetables, or maybe some wholemeal toast. Once the extreme hunger has abated then it's OK to have a biscuit or the occasional slice of cake. Stacking the house with junk food and tempting sweet treats is always going to cause strife, as you'll be constantly rationing and having to say no, but having the odd less healthy option available is also important. It's crucial to get some distance from the roller-coaster of extremes that young people are constantly fed on social media, from faddish superfood diets to fast food by the bucket.

A good relationship with food has to be about balance – plenty of natural, honest food and a few less nutritious, but truly delicious, bites too. Much of our enjoyment of food is linked to habits, traditions and food memories; our comfort food is so often a dish we ate as a youngster. Positive mealtimes, with a wide variety of home-cooked food, are the surest way to create a good appetite to last a lifetime.

Summer

Apricots, Artichokes, Asparagus, Aubergines, Beetroots,
Blackcurrants, Blueberries, Broad Beans, Broccoli, Chard,
Cherries, Courgettes, Cucumbers, Damsons, Fennel, Garlic,
Gooseberries, Greengages, Green Beans, Kohlrabi, Lettuce,
Mangetouts, New Potatoes, Peaches, Peas, Peppers, Plums,
Radishes, Raspberries, Redcurrants, Spring Onions,
Sweetcorn, Strawberries, Tomatoes, Turnips, Watercress

Green Salad: Just a Bowl of Leaves?

You may wonder whether a bowl of raw green leaves warrants all this chat. After all, it doesn't really require a recipe – just a good wash and a simple dressing. The trouble is that we seem to have lost interest in seeking out interesting salad greens; the plastic bags of, let's face it, bland mixed leaves are ubiquitous. It's rare nowadays to encounter a bowl of single-variety salad, and in fact it's wonderfully refreshing when you do.

There's such a fabulous variety of leaves out there: from blousy-soft butterheads to crispy romaines and from bitter radicchios to mustardy mizunas. It seems a shame to opt for the same old pre-mixes time after time.

Salad greens taste good when recently harvested, so it's worth seeking out a head of lettuce or a bag of loose, unwashed leaves from a local farm shop, greengrocer or market whenever you get the chance.

There will be times when convenience, or a lack of choice, pushes us towards the less economical choice of the pre-washed salad bag – but how about trying to break the habit? A medium gem lettuce weighs about the same as the average mixed salad bag and costs a fraction of the price; you're paying for all that extra transportation, washing, drying and packaging.

Preparing a head of lettuce takes just 5 minutes to strip off the leaves, rinse under cold running water in a colander and then spin-dry in a salad spinner if you have one (using the salad spinner basket as the colander reduces the faff too).

It's a good idea to prep a whole lettuce, or bag of leaves, even if you aren't using it all at once. Once washed and dried, place in a container lined with kitchen paper, leaving plenty of space. Cover with a lid or a slightly damp tea towel and you have prepped leaves for sandwiches or quick meals.

Over a third of the bagged, pre-washed salad that we buy is said to end up in the bin. How can that be?

Well, there's the bag that smells like a fetid pond as you open it, where some of the leaves have become slimy owing to excess moisture or bad storage. More often than not, we use half the bag and forget to use the rest. The problem is that once you've broken into the 'modified atmosphere packaging' that has, due to a lack of oxygen, kept your leaves in limbo for an extended time, they seem to go off very quickly. You're best to empty the remaining leaves into a container, lined with kitchen paper to absorb any moisture, and to use them within a couple of days.

How to Salvage Some Tired Lettuce or Use up Those Last Few Leaves

- If your leaves are looking a little sad and limp, soak them for 30 minutes in a bowl of really cold water. Some people even add a couple of ice cubes; the leaves will crisp up beautifully.

- A few stray leaves or a handful of lettuce can be added to a smoothie.

- Whizz the leaves in a blender with a little extra-virgin olive oil, lemon juice or vinegar and use on soups, pulses or grains as a dressing. You can add a few herbs, seeds and nuts too.

- Chopped leaves can be added to a stir-fry for the last few seconds – this works well with bigger leaves where you get a contrast between silky, collapsed leaf and crispy stem.

- Slice watercress stalks, or the central core of lettuces such as romaine, into wafer-thin pieces to add texture to salads and avoid waste.

A Few Salad Tips

A simple, single-variety salad is usually a winner as a side dish. Here are two different dressings to try.

FRENCH VINAIGRETTE

MAKES AROUND 60ML (4 TBSP)

- 3 tbsp extra-virgin olive oil
- 1 tbsp white wine vinegar
- 1 tsp Dijon mustard
- Pinch of caster sugar
- Salt and pepper, to taste

Place all the ingredients in a jam jar. Close the lid and shake to emulsify before serving.

Try cutting tight heads of gem lettuce, chicory or radicchio into wedges and chargrilling on a ridged griddle pan until lightly browned, before serving with the French vinaigrette and some grated Parmesan or a pesto and some warm lentils.

THAI DRESSING

MAKES AROUND 100ML (3½FL OZ)

- 4 tbsp lime juice
- 2 tbsp fish or soy sauce
- 2 tsp toasted sesame oil
- 2 tsp grated fresh root ginger
- 1–2 tsp caster sugar
- 1–2 chillies, finely chopped
- 1–2 garlic cloves, crushed

Mix together all the ingredients. Dress the lettuce and serve with finely sliced spring onions and chopped roasted peanuts.

This dressing is particularly good with super-crisp leaves such as Romaine, Iceberg or Chinese leaf.

KALE

Kale may have a bit of a worthy reputation when it comes to salad, but given the right treatment it makes a brilliant winter choice and can stand up to a few hours in the lunchbox without becoming slimy. Strip the leaf away from the stem/spine of the kale (the stalks can be finely sliced and stir-fried). Wash, then chop the leaves. Add a pinch of salt and a splash of extra-virgin olive oil to the kale and massage for 3–4 minutes until the leaves have tenderised and become a more vibrant green. Try with diced shallot, sliced apple, roasted hazelnuts and a splash of lemon juice.

There's so much more to salad than opening a bag of leaves.

Vegetable Fritters

Really quick to make, infinitely versatile and guaranteed to get even the most stubborn of vegetable doubters on board. These fritters just happen to be gluten free and egg free (and dairy free too, should you so choose). The range of pulse flours that is available has increased considerably; as well as chickpea flour (gram flour), try British pea and fava bean flours (page 17).

SERVES 4

2 tbsp olive oil, plus 2–3 tbsp for frying
1 onion, finely diced
3 garlic cloves, crushed
Spice of choice (see below), optional
200g (7oz) grated vegetables (see below)
A handful of fresh chopped herbs
1 tbsp seeds
Grated or crumbled cheese (see below), optional
100g (3½oz) British pea flour, fava bean flour or chickpea flour (gram flour)
1 tsp salt
1 tbsp water (optional)
Salad, pickle, pesto, whipped cheese or tahini, to serve

Heat the 2 tbsp oil in a large frying pan over a medium heat and fry the onion for 10 minutes, or until soft. Stir in the garlic and any spices (if using) and cook for 2 minutes. Leave to cool while you grate the vegetables.

In a large bowl, mix the onion with all the ingredients, except the olive oil for frying and the water, together well, massaging a little to bring the moisture out of the grated vegetables. If it seems very dry, add the water.

Heat the 2–3 tbsp olive oil for frying in a large frying pan and use a large spoon to place spoonfuls of the mixture into the hot oil. Flatten with the back of a spoon. Fry in 2 batches, turning the fritters after about 4 minutes on each side, once golden and set.

Drain on kitchen paper and keep warm in a low oven for a few minutes if not serving straight away. Serve with a fresh salad, pickle, pesto, whipped cheese or tahini.

Variations
Here are some great combinations. The onion, garlic, pulse flour and seasoning are the constants; everything else is a chance to play around.

1 tsp chilli flakes + courgette + 2 tbsp chopped basil + 1 tbsp chopped sun-dried tomatoes + 1 tbsp toasted pine kernels + 2 tbsp grated Parmesan. Serve with a salad of chopped tomatoes and capers.

1 tsp whole cumin seed + ½ tsp dried thyme + carrot + 1 tbsp chopped mint + 1 tbsp chopped black olives + toasted sesame oil + 4 tbsp crumbled feta. Serve with a drizzle of pomegranate molasses and whipped tahini.

1 tsp smoked paprika + ½ tsp ground cumin + pumpkin/squash + 2 tbsp chopped coriander + 2 tsp capers + 1 tbsp toasted pumpkin seeds + grated lime zest and juice.

Flatbreads

One of the quickest, cheapest and most satisfying things to make – you'll never give those supermarket packs of wraps a glance again. Cook to order, or pile them up in a foil parcel to keep them soft and then heat and eat later – they are best served warm.

A blend of mostly white and a little wholemeal flour gives the best of both worlds: a light, pliable bread with the nutty flavour and some healthy fibre from the whole grain.

MAKES 6 X 20CM (8-INCH) FLATBREADS

- 150g (5oz) plain white flour, plus extra for dusting
- 50g (1¾oz) wholemeal flour
- 2 tbsp extra-virgin olive oil
- ½ tsp salt
- 110–120ml (3¾–4fl oz) water, plus extra if needed
- 50g (1¾oz) ghee or butter, melted, or 50ml (2fl oz) extra-virgin olive oil, for brushing

FOLDED FLATBREADS – ADDING SPICES, SEEDS AND HERBS

Once you have your thin, rolled-out dough, brush lightly with ghee, butter or oil, then sprinkle with your chosen flavouring (see below). Be as creative as you like. Fold the top and bottom third of the dough in (as you would a letter), then fold over the sides to make a square. Roll out until you have thin dough and cook as above.

How about?
- Finely chopped rosemary and crushed garlic
- Dried thyme, oregano, sumac, toasted sesame, salt (for Middle Eastern za'atar)
- Roughly ripped wild garlic and coarsely ground black pepper

Pour the flours into a large bowl with the olive oil and salt. Slowly tip in the water, while stirring and bringing the dough together with one hand. You want a soft and slightly sticky mixture that leaves the bowl clean. If you are left with any dry flour in the bowl, add a splash more water.

Continue to work the dough with your hand, pushing it against the side of the bowl with your knuckles, before kneading it on a work surface for about 5 minutes; only add flour if it is impossibly sticky. Set the dough aside to relax for about 15 minutes.

Have a bowl of flour ready for dusting. Roll the dough into a log on a lightly floured surface and divide it into 6–8 pieces, depending on the size of your frying pan (a heavy, cast-iron pan works well). Shape the dough into small discs and dip into the flour to dust.

Roll out the dough discs to fit your pan, giving them regular quarter turns as you go; this keeps a circular shape and stops them from sticking.

Heat the pan until really hot, then cook the flatbread, in the dry pan one at a time, for 30 seconds, or until bubbles form on the surface. Flip the bread over with tongs, turning again after another 30 seconds. Cook for a further 1 minute, pressing down around the edges of the bread with a spatula to encourage the air into a large bubble in the centre of the dough – air pockets give a lighter bread.

Brush the flatbread with ghee, butter or olive oil and wrap in a foil parcel until ready to eat.

Bean Burgers

A dense texture with a bit of bite is the holy grail when it comes to a bean burger; there are far too many mushy recipes out there. The key is to dry out your cooked beans a little in a warm oven while you prepare your vegetables. The seeds take the place of eggs, binding the mixture together to give a more robust burger.

MAKES 4 BURGERS

400g (14oz) can red kidney beans, drained, or 250g (9oz) home-cooked
1 tbsp chia, flax- or camelina seeds (or 1 medium egg)
3 tbsp water
2 tbsp olive oil
1 onion, diced
1 red pepper, diced
2 garlic cloves, crushed
1 tbsp tomato purée
1 tsp ground cumin
Leaves from 3 sprigs of thyme
3 tbsp walnut pieces (or other nuts)
75g (2¾oz) mature Cheddar or Parmesan, finely grated, crumbled feta or vegan cheese
Finely grated zest of 1 lemon
75g (2¾oz) rolled oats or fresh breadcrumbs
1 tsp salt
Olive or rapeseed oil, for frying

Preheat the oven to 150°C/130°C fan/gas 2.

Put the beans onto a large baking tray, press them down with a potato masher to crush lightly, then put them into the oven for 15 minutes.

Crush the seeds with a pestle and mortar, then add the water and set aside to thicken. It will become rather gluey, but don't worry: this will help to bind the burgers.

Heat the olive oil in a small pan over a medium heat and fry the onion and red pepper for 10 minutes, or until soft. Add the garlic and cook for 2 minutes, or until fragrant.

Tip two-thirds of the beans into a large bowl and crush them with the back of a fork to a rough mash. Add the remaining beans, the fried vegetables, tomato purée, cumin, thyme, nuts, cheese, lemon zest (not the juice), oats, salt and the rather gloopy-looking seeds and mix well.

Shape the mixture into 4 burgers, about 2cm (¾ inch) thick, then place them on a baking tray in the fridge to firm up for about 1 hour (you can freeze them at this point too).

Heat a large, non-stick frying pan, add a little oil and fry the burgers, in batches if necessary, for about 3 minutes on each side until browned and crisp.

SERVE WITH
- Pink Onion Pickle or Instant Pickled Cucumber (page 47), kimchi or sauerkraut.
- Mayonnaise or Whipped Tahini (page 64), Babaganoush or Muhummara (page 131).
- Tomato, Nectarine, Mint and Feta Salad (page 147).
- In a roll, with a flatbread, or even between two leaves of crispy lettuce.

Smoky Peppers and Aubergines

If you're firing up the barbecue, or using the oven, during the summer months it makes sense to add a few peppers and aubergines to whatever else you are cooking. Their smoky, succulent flesh can be used for salads, for almost-instant pasta sauces, to top bruschetta or to whip up any number of Mediterranean dips (see opposite).

To Prepare

Choose smooth, shiny aubergines with drum-tight skin and red or yellow peppers (unless you are seeking out the more bitter flavours of the green).

Preheat the oven to between 180°C/160°C fan/gas 4 and 220°C/200°C fan/gas 7, if using, or heat the barbecue. Prick a few holes in the aubergines (so that they don't explode).

Place the whole vegetables over a hot barbecue flame, directly on the flame of a gas hob or under the hottest grill. The idea is to blacken and char the skin, giving a smoked flavour to the flesh underneath.

Place the blackened vegetables on a large baking tray and roast in the hot oven or wrap in a foil parcel and place on the barbecue until completely soft and tender. Depending on the size of the vegetables this will be about 20 minutes for peppers and up to 40 minutes for aubergines. (If you're slow-roasting the lamb on page 132, your vegetables can roast alongside but will take longer to soften).

Once cooked, cover the tray with an upturned bowl or leave in the foil parcel to cool. Then, once cool enough to handle, peel or scrape away the skin, remove the pepper seeds and store the roasted flesh in any juices. This will keep in the fridge for around 4 days (or a week if covered in a layer of oil).

Once you have the smoked vegetables you are ready to make any of the four following recipes.

ESCALIVADA – SPANISH CHARRED VEGETABLES

A versatile summer side dish that works just as well with Vegetable Fritters (page 126) and Bean Burgers (page 129) as it does with meat or fish. Escalivada can take centre stage too, as a topping for griddled toast or pan con tomate (page 142).

SERVES 4 AS A SIDE DISH OR 6 AS A TOPPING FOR TOASTED BREAD

- 3 small onions
- 3 smoky red peppers
- 3 smoky aubergines
- 2 garlic cloves, crushed
- 3 tbsp extra-virgin olive oil
- 2 tbsp sherry vinegar
- Pinch of salt

Roast the onions along with the other vegetables, and prepare (see left). Rip, or cut the aubergine, pepper and onion flesh into strips and place on a platter.

Mix the garlic, olive oil, vinegar and salt together in a bowl, then pour over the vegetables. Serve at room temperature.

Try this
- Add a few anchovies, black olives or capers for a punchier dish.
- Serve with a fresh goat's cheese or feta.

3 More Ways with Smoky Vegetables

These recipes are fabulous with pitta, on charred toast or as accompaniments to meat, fish or perhaps some fried halloumi.

ALL SERVE 4–6

MUHUMMARA – SYRIAN PEPPER AND WALNUT DIP

- 4 smoky red peppers (see opposite)
- 1–2 garlic cloves, roughly chopped
- 3 tbsp fresh breadcrumbs
- 50g (1¾oz) walnuts
- 1 tbsp Aleppo, Urfa or other mild chilli flakes
- 1 tbsp pomegranate molasses
- 1 tsp ground cumin
- 2 tbsp extra-virgin olive oil
- Juice of 1–2 lemons
- Salt, to taste

Blitz all the ingredients together in a food processor or blender to a rough paste. Add enough lemon juice and salt to make the sauce fresh and zingy. Store in the fridge for 3–4 days.

BABAGANOUSH – MIDDLE EASTERN AUBERGINE DIP

- 3 smoky aubergines (see opposite)
- 2 garlic cloves, roughly chopped
- Juice of 2–3 lemons
- 1–2 tbsp tahini
- 2–3 tbsp extra-virgin olive oil
- 1 tbsp cumin seeds, toasted
- 1 tbsp chopped parsley, 1 tbsp chopped coriander or 1 tbsp pomegranate seeds
- Salt and pepper

Blitz the aubergine flesh with the garlic, the juice of 2 lemons, 1 tbsp each of the tahini and olive oil and a pinch of salt and pepper in a blender or food processor. Taste and adjust the balance as necessary. Top with the toasted cumin seeds and your choice of herb or pomegranate seeds. Store in the fridge for 3–4 days.

ZAALOUK – MOROCCAN AUBERGINE AND TOMATO

- 2 tbsp extra-virgin olive oil, plus extra to taste
- 75g diced shallot
- 3 tbsp tomato purée
- 2 tsp cumin seeds
- 2 garlic cloves, crushed
- 3 smoky aubergines (see opposite), flesh roughly diced
- Juice of 2 lemons
- A handful of fresh coriander, chopped
- Salt and pepper

Heat the olive oil in a wide pan over a low heat and fry the shallot until soft. Add the tomato purée and cook until the colour deepens. Add the cumin, garlic and aubergine and cook for 5 minutes. Stir in the lemon juice and season, then add enough olive oil to give an indulgent texture. Stir in most of the coriander, reserving a few leaves to garnish. Store in the fridge for 3–4 days.

Party Food:
Slow-roasted Pulled
Shoulder of Lamb

Shoulder is not only one of the most economical cuts of lamb; it's packed with connective tissue that melts down to give the juiciest results imaginable. If you're feeding a crowd the pulled meat can be served in relatively small portions, almost as a garnish rather than the main player on the plate. The rich flavour works its magic with the chickpea recipe below and any of the smoky vegetable dishes on page 130.

SERVES 12 OR MORE, AS A RICH GARNISH

1 x 2kg (4½lb) shoulder of lamb
6 garlic cloves, halved
2 tbsp olive oil
1 sprig of rosemary, finely chopped
2 sprigs of thyme, finely chopped
5 onions, halved
100ml (3½fl oz) balsamic vinegar, plus extra to taste
100ml (3½fl oz) water
Salt and pepper

Preheat the oven to 200°C/180°C fan/gas 6.

Make 12 small incisions in the lamb shoulder and push in the garlic halves.

Rub 1 tbsp of the olive oil onto the lamb, then sprinkle with plenty of salt, pepper and the chopped herbs. Put the onion halves into a large roasting tin, drizzle with the remaining olive oil, then lay the lamb on top. Roast in the hot oven for 30 minutes, or until the meat begins to colour.

Reduce the oven temperature to 150°C/130°C fan/gas 2.

Add the vinegar and water to the roasting tin and cover with foil. Roast for 5 hours, or until the lamb easily comes away from the bone and can be shredded with two forks. Set the lamb aside for at least 30 minutes to rest, covered with the foil.

Meanwhile, skim off any excess fat from the roasting tin and add more vinegar, salt and pepper as required to balance.

Pull the meat apart with two forks and serve with the roasted onions and juices.

TRY THIS
Make use of the oven space
Roast your ready-charred peppers or aubergines until soft (page 130).

Oven-cooked chickpeas
Serves 12
Soak 500g (1lb 2 oz) chickpeas overnight. The next day, preheat the oven to 150°C/130°C fan/gas 2. Drain the chickpeas and place in a large ovenproof pan with a lid (or a roasting tin covered with foil), add about 2 litres (3½ pints) water and 2 bay leaves and cook in the oven for 3–4 hours until tender. Season and add 4 tbsp extra-virgin olive oil. To serve with the lamb, add the chickpeas to the roasted onions and lamb juices, stir in a handful of chopped sun-dried tomatoes, 100g (3½oz) pitted black olives and plenty of chopped parsley.

Food When You're Out and About

function, so we can't do our best thinking after a meal devoid of goodness and fibre.

Of course, there are exceptions to the rule, and a street food market can be the most fabulous way to explore new cuisines and flavours, meet artisan producers and eat some good and healthy food. There are some extraordinarily good delis and cafés creating great options too, but they may not be on your workplace's doorstep or affordable every day.

Investing in a few basic pieces of packed lunch kit is worth it in the long run. There's nothing worse than discovering that the salad dressing has leaked all over your handbag or your kid's schoolbooks. There are plenty of box options that are also pleasant to eat out of, such as bamboo bento boxes, or even the classic food-on-the-move container: the stainless-steel tiffin tin.

It's incredibly easy to snap up lunch, or a snack, pretty much anywhere – service stations, supermarkets, corner shops, fast-food joints; we're surrounded by businesses flogging takeaway food. But is this food doing us any good?

A large proportion of food on offer on the high street is calorie-rich, nutrient-poor, fast food. The truth is that those supermarket meal deals, made up of a sandwich, a bag of crisps or a sweet treat, along with a drink that could contain more sugar than the UK's recommended daily allowance, are a disaster if eaten on a daily basis.

Highly processed, low-nutrient food can lead to weight gain, as we eat more of it because it doesn't fill us up for long. Being overweight can increase our odds of suffering from type 2 diabetes, heart disease, stroke and cancer. If that's not bad enough, what we eat affects how we perform; unstable blood sugar can be detrimental to brain

So... 5 reasons to bother with a lunchbox

- **Variety and taste** Sandwich, salad, soup, stew? You can play around with an infinite number of combinations using your favourite ingredients.
- **Healthier** You know exactly what's going in, and can pack it with whole foods that will keep you energised for longer.
- **Cheaper** Once you have some base ingredients in place, and particularly when making multiple lunches, you can create great food on a budget.
- **Waste less** Packed lunches can be a great way to use up last night's leftovers.
- **Packaging free** No more plastic containers, sandwich boxes or disposable cutlery.

The Hot Packed Lunch

Whole foods, and pulses in particular, provide the perfect bedrock for a packed lunch, filling you up with slow-release energy to keep you going for the rest of the day.

Dishes such as:
- Baked Beans and all the variations (page 39)
- Minestrone (page 67)
- Dal (page 44)
- Creamed Vegetable Soup, and throw in some extra beans to fill you up (page 62)
- Mushroom and Lentil Ragu (page 158)
- A veggie noodle soup

… with maybe a flatbread, a hunk of bread or a few oatcakes on the side, and a piece of fresh fruit and perhaps a small pot of granola to finish.

If you're carrying this in a food flask then it's worth remembering that only wet food will stay really hot; you can always top up drier mixes with hot stock. Heat the flask by adding boiling water and setting aside with a lid on while you get the food piping hot. Tip away the water, add the food and close the lid straight away.

When filling a food flask with curries, stews and salads a jam funnel is especially handy, making spills and overflows a thing of the past.

Avoid high-risk foods such as rice, seafood and meat, which might not stay at quite a high enough temperature, to avoid spoilage and the risk of food poisoning.

Insulated bags can be a great idea for children taking lunch to school, or for adults if there's no fridge available at work. Food flasks, which keep food both hot or cold for a number of hours, are ideal for school kids, or anyone with no access to heating-up or chilling facilities.

The Cold Lunch Box

Just don't call it a salad – otherwise half the household will have decided that it's not filling enough, or not their thing, before you've even made the dressing.

Beans and grains benefit from sitting in a dressing overnight, supping up all the flavours, while it's usually more appetising to scatter the vegetables on top, to stir in later when you're ready to eat.

Try the Bulgur, Butter Bean and Summer Greens Salad (page 139) or the Smoked Quinoa, Kale and Apple Salad (page 30).

Here's a template for a satisfying cold lunch

300g (10½oz) cooked whole grain, e.g. freekeh, bulgur wheat, maftoul, quinoa, whole or pearled spelt or any other whole 'berry'.
+
125g (4½oz) cooked pulses, such as beans, chickpeas or lentils (½ a drained can).
+
200g (7oz) vegetables, such as raw or roasted vegetables (great for using up leftovers from a roast). Tomatoes are best left whole, otherwise they become a bit woolly, so use cherries. Avoid tender-leaf lettuces that can become rather slimy.
+
20g (¾oz) toasted nuts, seeds, crumbled cheese or chopped dried fruit.
+
Dressing, such as French Vinaigrette (page 125), Pesto (page 93), Chimichurri (page 93) and Salsa Verde (page 139).

The Baffling World of Bottled Water

Are you old enough to remember the novelty of travelling abroad and finding the bottle of water on the table an unfamiliar, and even rather exotic, sight?

Nowadays, many think nothing of snapping up their daily bottle of water with a supermarket meal deal, in a café at lunchtime, or from a convenience store as a rehydration fix with a snack. The fact that British tap water is perfectly safe to drink means that we could all embrace saving money, as well as, quite crucially, reducing the terrifying quantities of plastic bottles being produced.

A bottle of water may seem cheap when compared with other drinks, but in reality you are paying for the bottle itself and for its distribution, sales and marketing and retail profits, while the water costs well under a tenth of a per cent of the price. Manufacturing the bottle, bottling the water, labelling and transporting all take energy. In fact, studies have shown that bottled water uses about 2000 times the amount of energy to reach you than tap water, and that's even before considering the other massive problem: plastic waste pollution.

Globally around 1 million plastic bottles are sold every minute, and well under a quarter of those are ever recycled. Even in the UK, where so many of us pride ourselves on our diligent sorting of rubbish for recycling, much of that plastic ends up in incinerators or is exported to be dealt with in other countries. We are quite literally exporting our problem, transferring our rubbish to other communities who are often even less equipped to deal with it in an environmentally acceptable way. Plastic that winds up in landfill will take centuries to break down while it leaches toxins into our soils and water systems. Perhaps more troubling are the bottles that make up a third of all plastic pollution in the sea. If marine plastic pollution continues to rise at its

current rate, the amount of plastic in the sea will outweigh fish by 2050.

There are murmurs of hope from Japan, where scientists are working with a strain of bacteria that is capable of decomposing plastic; how amazing that could be on an industrial scale. Meanwhile, we have to reduce our plastic consumption; recycling alone is not the answer.

What Can We Do?

Keep a reusable water bottle in your bag at all times; it will soon become second nature. Carrying a water bottle is hardly difficult; it's just about getting into the habit and getting to know where you can refill it. All National Trust cafés offer free drinking water, so do bring your own bottle to refill during your visit. There are even refill apps available (page 184), so that you can locate a refill station or obliging café when you are out and about.

Let's push community centres, sports venues and transport hubs to make free drinking water more readily accessible. Petition supermarkets to offer water on tap rather than bottles as part of their meal deal offers, perhaps with a financial incentive to encourage shoppers to choose to refill.

Drink More Tap Water

Many of us fail to function on full throttle because we are slightly dehydrated. If you find yourself or family members struggling to drink enough water, it may be time to make it more of a tempting option.

If your tap water tastes like a swimming pool you could use a filter jug, place a simple charcoal filter in your bottle or invest in some kind of filter tap – you'll save money in the long term if you stop buying bottled water, and be looking after the environment.

It's probably worth getting a soda stream or similar appliance if you enjoy carbonated water, reducing both packaging and the weight of the shopping you have to lug home.

Keeping a reusable bottle or a jug of chilled drinking water topped up in the fridge makes it more appealing.

Add fresh mint or a sprig of rosemary, a slice of citrus, ribbons of cucumber (or just the cucumber seeds, if you are removing them from another dish). A few slices of ripe stone fruit or some lightly crushed fresh berries left for a few hours to macerate will gently flavour the water.

Homemade cordials such as Elderflower Cordial (page 90) are additive free but do contain sugar, as we can't be angels all of the time.

When it comes to hot drinks, try adding a few slithers of fresh ginger, a stick of lemongrass quartered lengthways, a few dried hibiscus petals or some mint or lemon verbena leaves for a much fresher tasting, and cheaper, option than commercial herbal teas. Try making your own Nettle Tea (page 90).

Other Drinks

Tea and coffee both offer so many benefits, and some downsides. On the one hand, they give us huge pleasure, a lift in energy and are at the centre of so many rituals and traditions, but in excess, they may leave us buzzing with anxiety or virtually levitating in bed with a caffeine rush. It's all about balance and knowing your limits.

The same can be said for alcohol, associated with enjoyment, relaxation and celebration but also a dangerous substance that can lead to addiction and a reduced quality and length of life. It's a question of savouring alcohol, if you do drink, rather than binge drinking or downing it on a daily basis.

The one family of drinks that are often mistakenly considered pretty benign, and handed out freely to so many of our kids, are fizzy drinks, and yet apart from hydration they offer nothing positive for health. Typically sweetened with high-fructose corn syrup, they're usually loaded with additives and their regular consumption is closely correlated with obesity and responsible for appalling levels of tooth decay. High-sugar energy drinks, fizzy drinks and even commercial flavoured waters, shouldn't be considered an alternative to water but instead an occasional treat.

Bulgur, Butter Bean and Summer Greens Salad with Salsa Verde

This salad is equally good eaten straight away while slightly warm on a chilly evening or made in advance for tomorrow's lunchbox. The combination of nutritious grains and pulses, vegetables and nuts makes for a very satisfying meal. You can also add some griddled halloumi, boiled eggs or flakes of cooked salmon on top, if you like.

SERVES 4 AS A MAIN OR 6 AS A SIDE

150g (5oz) coarse bulgur wheat
2 x 400g (14oz) cans butter beans, or 500g/1lb 2oz home-cooked (or 1 large jar)
2 tbsp extra-virgin olive oil
1 garlic clove, crushed
2–3 medium courgettes (about 400g/14oz)
300g (10½oz) runner beans, French beans, such as Helda, or Bobby beans, trimmed
60g (2¼oz) roasted almonds
Salt and pepper

Salsa verde
1 large bunch of parsley
12 mint or basil leaves, or both
1 garlic clove, crushed
2 tbsp capers, drained
6 anchovy fillets (or 6 green pitted olives if you prefer)
1 tbsp Dijon mustard
3 tbsp red wine vinegar
6 tbsp extra-virgin olive oil
Salt and pepper

Begin by making the salsa verde, chopping the herbs, garlic, capers and anchovies quite roughly so that you have some good texture, rather than a green paste. Stir in the mustard, vinegar and olive oil and add pepper (and salt as required, but the anchovies and capers are both salty). The salsa should have plenty of attitude; you have a lot of grains and beans to season.

Cook the bulgur wheat according to the packet instructions (some finer-textured varieties need no more than a quick soak in boiling water, while the coarser, cracked grains may require some cooking). Once ready, place in a large bowl and stir in about half of the salsa verde while the grains are still warm.

Drain the butter beans and warm through in a saucepan with the olive oil, garlic and a pinch of salt, just long enough to smell the garlic. Remove from the heat and leave the beans to steep. This trick is a brilliant way to give canned beans another dimension before using in any salad, absorbing the warm garlicky oil as they sit.

Slice the courgettes lengthways into thin ribbons, about 5mm (¼ inch) thick, and season with plenty of salt and pepper. Heat a ridged griddle pan and cook the strips for 3–5 minutes on each side until they are charred and soft. Place in a bowl and toss with the remaining salsa verde while still warm.

Steam the green beans for 3–4 minutes until tender.

Carefully tumble the butter beans in with the bulgur, then pile the tangle of courgettes and green beans on top. Sprinkle over the roasted almonds and serve slightly warm or at room temperature.

Mackerel with Rhubarb Salsa

Many of us rarely eat oily fish even though it is delicious and contains the essential omega-3 fatty acids that are vital for heart and brain health. Fresh mackerel can be an absolute bargain in the summer months, and especially if you live near the coast; be sure to ask your fishmonger for the more sustainable, line-caught fish. The fish on offer will, and should, vary with the weather, so be flexible: sardines, sprats or even trout will also work well.

The rhubarb salsa is a revelation; the acidity cuts through the richness of the fish beautifully.

SERVES 4

4 fresh mackerel, filleted
2 tbsp plain flour
2 tbsp rapeseed or
   vegetable oil
Salt and pepper
Potato salad, new
   potatoes or mashed
   potatoes, to serve
   (optional)

Rhubarb salsa
200g (7oz) rhubarb, cut
   into 2cm (¾ inch) logs
1 small red onion, diced
Finely grated zest and
   juice of 1 orange
1 red chilli, finely sliced
1 tsp finely grated fresh
   root ginger
1 tsp caster sugar
Pinch of salt

For the salsa, place all the salsa ingredients in a large frying pan, cover with a lid and simmer gently for 5–10 minutes until the rhubarb is just beginning to soften. Remove from the heat and spoon the salsa into a small bowl. The idea is to keep the rhubarb intact; it will continue to soften as it cools. Set aside.

Check the mackerel fillets for bones. There are often a couple of stubborn pin bones at the top end of the fillet that you can remove with tweezers.

Spread the flour out on a large plate and season with salt and pepper. Dip the skin side of each fillet into the seasoned flour to lightly dust it. Heat 1 tbsp of the oil in a large, non-stick frying pan and fry 2 fillets, skin-side down, for 2–4 minutes, pressing down gently with a fish slice to cook the skin evenly. Once the skin is crisp and golden, turn the fish over and cook for a further minute, or until the flesh is just opaque. Remove and cook the remaining 2 fillets with the rest of the oil.

Serve the fillets with the tangy salsa and perhaps some potato salad, new potatoes or mash.

TRY THIS
- If finding fresh fish is tricky, how about using some readily available canned fish? Quite simply open a can of sardines, grill them on toast and top with the salsa.
- The salsa is heaven as a dal topping or with canned sardines, pulled pork or Peking duck too.

Every Last Crumb: Tackling Bread Waste

Toast for breakfast, sandwich for lunch, mid-afternoon tea cake, soup and croutons for supper; we consume a vast amount of bread in this country and we throw away truly shocking quantities of the stuff. The equivalent of a million loaves is wasted every day in the UK. When you consider the energy and water required to grow the grain, to harvest, transport and process it, to prepare and bake the bread and finally to bring it to market, that's quite a footprint to casually cast aside to the bin. Much of that wasted bread finishes up in landfill, creating yet more greenhouse gases.

Environmentalists and entrepreneurs are working on ways to get some of the surplus bread that doesn't even leave the shop shelf back into the food chain: looping it back into bakeries to cultivate starters or to be ground down as an ingredient in the next loaf, or using it to brew beer or create animal feed. We may even be manufacturing our clothes from yesterday's loaf in the future, as scientists are currently investigating making cotton-like fibres from fungi grown on old bread.

Meanwhile, back at home, we're throwing away good money, as well as contributing to the food waste mountain, when we discard old bread.

How to Use your Loaf

If consuming a loaf in a couple of days is a challenge, why not slice half of it and freeze it, ready for toast? Layering the slices at an angle in a freezer bag, rather like a row of fallen dominoes, makes pulling the frozen slices apart easier. No need to thaw before toasting.

Storing bread in a canvas bag as they do in Europe, rather than in a clammy bread bin, means that your bread will dry out rather than go mouldy – and there are countless ways to use dry or **stale bread**.

- A slightly leathery slice of good bread is perfect for a ridged griddle pan with a brush of olive oil; you can even top it with a few Italian ingredients and call it bruschetta. The Spanish rub hot toast with a garlic clove and squash over some tomato flesh, adding salt and olive oil, for a frugal, yet glorious, pan con tomate.
- The firm texture of stale toast is perfect for a classic croûte to top French onion soup or a Mediterranean-style fish stew (page 169).
- Bread can be toasted for quick croutons for soups (page 64) or ripped into a salad, such as the Panzanella opposite.
- Dry bread comes in handy for desserts too, soaking up the custard in classic bread and butter pudding or absorbing the deep pink berry juices in a Summer Pudding (page 144).

Finally, we come to the **crumbs**: every kitchen should have a good supply.

- To make fresh crumbs, break stale bread into chunks, blitz it in a food processor and store in the freezer. Essential in dishes such as stuffings, treacle tart, meatballs or white sauce.
- For finer, dried crumbs, ideal for crumbing food prior to frying, dry out the bread fully in a warm oven preheated to 150°C/130°C fan/gas 2 before blitzing.

Panzanella Salad

A fabulous Italian way to use up dry bread – and we're certainly not talking the mass-produced sliced stuff here – a good rustic white, ciabatta or sourdough will be perfect. While the tomatoes must be filled with flavour they can be a little past their best, too – a great moment to snap up some bargain 'vegetables on the edge' from a local supplier or to use up a glut.

SERVES 4–6

About 200g (7oz) stale bread
750g (1lb 10oz) ripe tomatoes, roughly chopped
1 small red onion, finely sliced
1–2 garlic cloves, crushed
A large handful of fresh basil leaves, torn
100ml (3½fl oz) extra-virgin olive oil
2–3 tbsp red wine vinegar
½ tsp caster sugar (optional)
Salt and pepper

Rip the bread, including the crusts, into small chunks and place in large bowl.

Now add all the remaining ingredients, seasoning well; it really couldn't be easier. If your tomatoes lack that extra bit of Mediterranean sweetness, a tiny sprinkle of sugar can work wonders. Set aside at room temperature for 2 hours for the flavours to get acquainted before serving.

TRY THIS

Add any of the following, keeping in mind the balance of the dish – the last four suggestions are all quite salty and intense.

- 2 roasted red or yellow peppers, skinned and sliced into ribbons.
- ½ cucumber, diced.
- 2 celery sticks, sliced.
- A small fennel bulb, finely sliced.
- A few sunblush tomatoes.
- 2 tbsp salted capers, rinsed.
- 12 black olives, stoned.
- 100g (3½oz) salted anchovies, rinsed in cold water and finely chopped.

Summer Pudding

This pudding is another opportunity to use up some slightly stale bread; white is the classic choice but wholemeal works well too.

The berries are up to you; slightly squashy overripe fruit is just fine and, although some might frown on the inclusion of strawberries, cherries or blackberries, it's really down to taste and what's available. It's a lot of fruit, so best wait for lower prices in the late summer or even visit a pick-your-own farm. Frozen mixed berries are often a more economical option, but do take care not to overcook them and end up with mush.

This pudding is best made the day before serving so that the bread has time to soak up the juices and holds together better. When it comes to turning out, a flexible plastic pudding basin is helpful, or you could line a ceramic basin with cling film.

SERVES 6–8

About 7–8 slices of stale bread, crusts removed (great for breadcrumbs)
900g (2lb) mixed berries, traditionally raspberries, redcurrants and blackcurrants
120g (4oz) light muscovado sugar, plus extra if needed
50ml (2fl oz) water
Whipped cream or ice cream, to serve

Cut a circle of bread to fit the bottom of a 1 litre (1¾ pint) pudding basin, press it in, then line the walls, overlapping the slices and pressing them together to seal. You should still have a little bread left over for the lid.

Heat the fruit, sugar and water together in a large saucepan for 2 minutes, or until the juices begin to bleed and the sugar dissolves. If using frozen fruit, only add about half of the fruit to the pan, then stir in the remaining fruit off the heat, otherwise your filling will be in danger of collapsing to a mush. Taste, as you may need more sugar; that's all down to your choice of fruit.

Spoon the warm berries into the bread-lined basin, reserving a few tablespoons of the juice, then top with a layer of bread.

Stand the pudding basin on a dish and cover with a saucer or plate that just fits inside the rim, pop a heavy weight on top and refrigerate overnight.

Just before serving, slide a palette knife around the inside of the basin and turn it out onto a plate with a lip that can hold the juice. If the pudding sticks stubbornly in its bowl, then give it a sharp shake and leave it for a moment for gravity to do its work. Tip the reserved juice over the pudding, focusing on any spots where the juice failed to seep through.

TRY THIS
Try substituting summer berries with an autumnal mix of blackberries and eating apples (cookers such as Bramleys are too wet). Peel, core and chop the apples, and cook the fruit for a little longer until the apples are tender, then prepare as above.

The Fruit Bowl

There's nothing better than perfectly ripe fruit to round off a meal and, while fruits do obviously contain sugars, they're generally in much lower quantities than in sweetened snacks, puddings and cakes. Calorie-counting consumers often ignore the fact that, even if their homemade fruit salad does contain the same 300 calories as a low-fat, processed cupcake, one is loaded with vital vitamins, minerals, phytochemicals and fibre while the other is just a carb fest, virtually devoid of nutrients.

As with all our food, eating a diverse selection is always a good idea. Rather than taking your trusty banana to work in the lunchbox, day after day, swap it with another piece of fruit whenever you can. Following the 'Eat the Rainbow' mantra makes good sense too, as consuming a variety of different-coloured fruits ensures that you're getting a wide spectrum of the vital minerals, essential vitamins and the phytochemicals available. Phytochemicals – the active compounds found in all plants – are now thought to help protect our cells and DNA from damage, reduce inflammation and even balance our hormones.

Rather than getting caught up in the hype about one superhero fruit's antioxidant qualities

or another's double load of vitamin C, you're probably best to go with what's ripe, tastes wonderful, is affordable, and, when possible, is local too.

Keep it Whole

Fruit is best eaten as a whole food, since the structure (and often the skin) give us the valuable fibre that:

- Slows down absorption of sugars (levelling out the blood-sugar highs and lows and our moods).
- Gives the digestive system a workout, making us feel full for longer.
- Feeds our gut bacteria, which in turn affects our overall health and well-being.
- Keeps us regular.

Fruit juices in particular, where the fibre has been removed completely, aren't great news, especially in the case of processed juices where they are often made from concentrate and may even have added sugars.

Smoothies are better than juice in this respect, but the fibre has still been broken down, leading to faster sugar absorption and then the associated dipping mood and energy levels soon after. The other problem, for those trying to maintain or lose weight, is that we may gulp a smoothie down in less than a minute and forget to think of it as a food. To counter this, try serving smaller glasses and balancing smoothies up with more vegetables, such as spinach, courgettes or cucumber, which don't over-impact the flavour, and never use sugary fruit juice to loosen the mixture – water is fine.

Best of all for our health is to eat fruit as naturally as possible – munching an apple just as it is, diving into a bowl of strawberries, or perhaps chopping up a selection of seasonal fruit for a salad.

Simple and Extraordinarily Good Ways with Fruit

Good fruit requires little help, but so often it languishes in the fruit bowl because we're too lazy or busy to get around to a bit of peeling or chopping. Here are a few ideas.

WINTER CITRUS SALAD

Peel and slice, or segment, a selection of oranges, blood oranges, mandarins, tangerines or grapefruit. In a pan, heat 50g (1¾oz) caster sugar in 100ml (3½fl oz) water with a sprig of rosemary and stir until the sugar dissolves. Remove from the heat and leave to cool and infuse. Add as much of the syrup to the fruit as you require, depending on the acidity of your fruit.

STRAWBERRIES AND ELDERFLOWER CORDIAL

Hull and halve your strawberries, then pour over a splash of Elderflower Cordial (page 90). Turn the fruit carefully in the cordial, taking care not to bruise it, then leave to macerate for 30 minutes. Sprinkle with a few frothy elderflowers and serve with cream. Poached rhubarb makes a sensational addition to this combination too.

NECTARINE, RASPBERRY, THYME AND TOASTED ALMONDS

Stone the nectarine(s) and cut into eighths, add raspberries, a sprinkling of fresh thyme leaves, a pinch of light muscovado sugar and a tiny splash of balsamic vinegar. Top with toasted flaked almonds and serve with mascarpone.

TOMATO, NECTARINE, MINT AND FETA

A showstopping combination if your fruit is at peak ripeness. Tumble together segments of tomato and nectarine with salt, pepper, extra-virgin olive oil and a splash of balsamic vinegar. Sprinkle with young mint leaves and crumbled feta just before serving.

LOCAL APPLE PLATTER

Serve a selection of heritage apples, cored and sliced, dunked quickly in lemon juice to stop browning, with a sprinkling of chopped dates and walnut halves. Add some tangy Cheddar and suddenly dessert becomes a light lunch, with a hunk of bread, or an interesting finale to a meal.

PEARS WITH SHEEP'S CHEESE AND HONEY

Serving slices of pear with pecorino is an Italian tradition but you could choose a local sheep's cheese, soft or hard – that's your shout. Serve with a fabulous honey and a good grind of pepper.

UNDER THE GRILL

Some fruits, such as plums and apricots, explode with flavour when they are heated. You can quite simply halve them and place them under a hot grill with a very light sprinkling of sugar. Serve warm with a spoonful of Granola (page 24) and ice cream.

For a truly delicious pudding, try crushing some amaretti biscuits to rough crumbs, mixing with a few drops of sweet wine or sweet sherry and placing the mixture in the stone cavity of the fruit. Sprinkle over a pinch of caster sugar and add a tiny knob of butter to each fruit. Grill until golden. Serve warm with Greek-style yogurt, mascarpone or cream.

STEWING

Simple stewing may not sound particularly promising, but a few minutes in a pan with a splash of water, cordial, fruit juice or wine can work wonders with slightly unripe or disappointing fruit. Add vanilla, cinnamon, cardamom or ginger. Be experimental; you could create a masterpiece.

Local Seasonal Fruit

Eating seasonal, local fruit as often as possible is important when it comes to looking after the environment. Having said that, the British fruit season does leave us struggling in the late spring when it can be a case of rhubarb, rhubarb, rhubarb and the odd apple – so try freezing or preserving local fruit in the times of plenty.

We import over 90 per cent of the fruit we consume in the UK, so avoiding imports altogether is impossible, but all imports are not equal when it comes to the environment. We can no longer turn a blind eye to fruit that is flown around the globe (along with other perishable ingredients); the resulting carbon emissions and their effect on climate change are just too huge to ignore.

It would be depressing to imagine never eating another pineapple or mango again, but what we can do is limit such treats to special occasions rather than mindlessly snapping up a portion from the supermarket as part of a daily meal deal (ready-prepped fruit tends to be flown in). Let's celebrate exotic fruits when we have them, maybe seeking out the perfect Indian Alphonso mango as they come into season in the spring or making that pineapple a late-winter treat when there's not much homegrown fruit on offer.

Shipped and road-freighted fruit does have a much smaller footprint – which is a relief, since bananas and oranges make up almost half of all the fruit we consume in Britain, and we obviously don't have the climate to grow them. Mediterranean citrus cheers us on through the depths of winter while Spanish and Italian stone fruits, such as peaches, nectarines and apricots, herald the beginning of summer.

As for our own, locally grown fruit, we should snap it up. We start the year with rhubarb (not, botanically speaking, a fruit, but we treat it as one), then strawberries, raspberries, cherries, gooseberries, red- and blackcurrants, plums, greengages, damsons, blackberries, apples, pears and quince. We have a pretty good run from May through to the end of the year and yet the shops are still filled with imported papayas, passion fruit and pineapples.

Supporting Local Farmers

Summer and autumn are the times to support our own fruit farmers, and particularly the smaller-scale producers who can't fulfil huge supermarket contracts. Research has shown that the nutritional value of fruit and vegetables held in cold storage for extended periods as they travel begins to diminish. That intoxicating smell of fresh strawberries, at the farmer's market or local greengrocer, speaks volumes; it's a sign of ripe fruit, picked at the right moment – and a sign that the flavour will beat the socks off most imports.

It seems inconceivable that we're often buying fruit from the other side of the planet when we have wonderful produce right on our doorstep. There's something awry when we're forking out for Chilean blueberries (yes, we grow our own here too) while our hedgerows are loaded with blackberries that are free.

It's time to reconnect with our own fruit growers. One fun way is to visit a pick-your-own farm, stocking up with fruit to make jam or freeze for a later date. Local markets are good places to find unusual varieties. It's sometimes about embracing food shopping as a fun and rewarding thing to do – a pleasant way to spend free time, rather than a chore.

Traditional Fruits

We've lost 90 per cent of our traditional orchards in the UK since the 1950s and now import a vast majority of our apples, even though we have the perfect growing climate. Two of our top-selling apples, Pink Lady and Granny Smith, aren't even

grown here. So why not seek out some of the hundreds of heritage apple varieties available in farm shops, markets and greengrocers in the autumn?

Traditional orchards are also havens for biodiversity, offering trees, grassland floor, scrub, fallen wood and hedgerow boundaries for our wildlife to flourish. Take a spring walk through an orchard in full blossom and you'll find that the air is alive with bees and other insects. So when you tuck in to an Ashmead's Kernel or an Egremont Russet it's a win-win; you can enjoy a unique flavour *and* the knowledge that you're supporting a precious ecosystem. The farmers need our support to keep on growing, so we need to provide a reliable market. When our supermarkets do take the punt on selling unfamiliar varieties, or less uniform-looking fruits, it's our chance to snap them up, sending a message to buyers that we're up for more diversity and variety.

The same can be said for our pears, plums and other stone fruit too. Once you've tasted a ripe plum, picked from a tree, its 'ripen-at-home' bargain bullet of a cousin will always be a disappointment.

Extraordinarily, it's common nowadays to see fruit rotting on trees in domestic gardens – fruit that no one can be bothered to pick. If you're lucky enough to have a tree, then get bartering if you can't eat the fruit yourself; you may get a few jars of jam, or a bunch of garden flowers, in return. Meanwhile, if you're on the lookout for fruit it can be worth posting on a neighbourhood chat forum or local social media group asking if anyone has any fruit that they'd like to sell – you'll often find that people are only too glad for someone else to come and do the picking.

Autumn

Apples, Aubergines, Beetroots, Blackberries, Broccoli, Brussels Sprouts, Carrots, Cauliflowers, Celeriac, Celery, Chestnuts, Courgettes, Damsons, Fennel, Figs, Garlic, Greengages, Jerusalem Artichokes, Kale, Leeks, Parsnips, Pears, Peppers, Plums, Potatoes, Pumpkins, Quinces, Squashes, Sweetcorn, Swiss Chard, Swedes, Turnips, Wild Mushrooms

Stocking up the Freezer

Historically we've spent the late summer and autumn preserving the gluts of fruit and vegetables to last us through the winter and early spring; nowadays, with fresh ingredients available all year round, we often forget that food is even seasonal. It's the great time of plenty and even if you are not a great bottler, jam-maker or pickler (although the Pink Onion Pickle on page 47 might inspire you), you can certainly use the freezer.

Apples, pears, plums and damsons tend to arrive in almost unmanageable quantities if you are lucky enough to have a fruit tree, or a neighbour with one. (It's even worth putting out a call on a local neighbours' group offering to pay for fruit if you're keen.) Apart from bottling and preserving, which take a degree of dedication and time, how about making some quick purées?

FRUIT PURÉE BULLETS

These are perfect stirred (straight from the freezer) into hot porridge or rice pudding, or even used in savoury sauces.

Peel and core apples or pears, remove the stones from plums and damsons and roughly chop the fruit. Add the fruit to a saucepan with 1cm (½ inch) water in the bottom and a touch of sugar (keep the purées fairly tart so that you can use them in both sweet and savoury recipes). Cover the pan and simmer the fruit for 10 minutes, or until just soft and collapsed. Blend until smooth, then freeze in ice-cube trays or silicone mini muffin/friand trays.

Great combinations: blackberry and apple, pear and stem ginger, plum and cardamom, damson and rosemary. Earlier in the year there are gooseberries and elderflower, rhubarb and star anise.

Foraged blackberries, elderberries and sloes can be frozen, ready to use in a simple hedgerow crumble or the flaxseed jam on page 33.

CITRUS

Next time you are squeezing a lemon or lime, grate the zest first. Little pots of lemon, lime and orange zest in the freezer, that you add to as you go, can be fabulous to use in baking, risottos, stews and soups.

Frozen citrus is a treat in a drink, doing the icing and slicing in one fell swoop. It's also a great way to preserve the other half of a used lemon.

EMPTY THE FRUIT BOWL

Freezing chopped fresh fruit is ideal if you enjoy a chilled smoothie occasionally, and a great way of clearing the fruit bowl if you've overcatered or you don't have time to clear the decks before going on holiday.

Bananas freeze brilliantly; it's the perfect way to deal with a bunch that have ripened too quickly. Slice the banana before freezing, ready for smoothies and **almost-instant banana ice cream**. Just blitz the frozen banana in a food processor until smooth and creamy. Use immediately or freeze again. Try adding chocolate chips, grated lime zest or a splash of vanilla extract. Dark, overripe bananas can be frozen in their skins ready for baking – try the Banana, Cardamom and Dark Chocolate Bites on page 116.

Frozen Vegetable Purées

Next time you are making a soup or a mashed vegetable side dish, think double. Your fried onion and leek base with cooked root vegetables, greens or pulses will freeze beautifully and is another meal in the making. It's best to freeze this as a dense, thick mixture, so that it takes up less space, and then add any stock or dairy when you reheat.

Ice-cube trays or small moulds are useful for freezing smaller quantities, such as for baby food. Omit the salt but include gentle spicing and herbs, in order to widen your child's taste experience.

Pulses take a while to cook, using up valuable energy and time. It's always worth cooking a large batch and freezing some for soups and stews at a later date. Portions of dal are brilliant for quick midweek meals that you can add fresh vegetables and herbs to before serving.

Herbs can be expensive and spoil quickly. Chop leftover leaves, place in ice-cube trays or silicone moulds and cover with olive oil or water. Freeze, then pop out and store in bags. Curry leaves and makrut lime leaves are always best fresh or frozen and kept in the freezer, along with lemongrass and fresh root ginger.

Stock

Having an ongoing bag in the freezer for vegetable offcuts, onion peels, parsley stalks and odd celery sticks is a great way to reduce waste and make frugal stocks (page 102). Once the stock has been prepared and strained, boil it to reduce the liquid by at least half so that you have more flavour and less volume to store.

Batch Cooking

Having a couple of homemade 'ready meals' in the freezer is always handy. Stews, chillies, ragus and soups freeze well, while dishes with a very high-fat content don't. Base recipes, such as the Mushroom and Lentil Ragu (page 158), are useful as you can use them in different ways – with pasta, in a pie, as a chilli or with a baked potato.

Freezer Tips

Ensure that your freezer is running at −18°C/0°F, or below.

Label, Label, Label

Be sure that the freezer is not just another stepping stone between the fridge and the rubbish bin. Freezing leftovers is a great plan as long as they're well labelled. That unidentified frozen object, or UFO, is never going to be an appetising supper option and will probably get thrown away in the annual freezer clear-out.

Freezer labels (which don't leave a residue on your containers) are available online, but masking tape can work well, along with a permanent marker pen. Don't forget to add the date as well as the name of the dish.

Containers

- Reuse takeaway containers and store with their lids on; every food service company makes a point of using a slightly different size! Wash and reuse zip-lock bags.

- Wide-necked, glass jars can be reused as long as the food is cold when it goes into the freezer and you leave 2cm (¾ inch) of space at the top of the jar for the food to expand.

- When reusing containers (both glass and plastic), either wash thoroughly in hot water or ideally run through a dishwasher to disinfect.

- Allow the food to thaw gradually if using a glass container – sudden changes in temperature could cause the glass to break.

- If buying new, sturdy glass containers with fitting lids that can be used in both the oven and freezer, are a good idea. Just buy them all the same size so that you always have the right lid.

Regular Audits

Frozen food does not retain its texture, taste or nutrients indefinitely. A monthly check through the contents ensures that you don't discover food after a decade and end up throwing it out. In general, in order to eat things at their best, freeze for:

- **Up to 3 months** for bread, cakes, cooked meals, soups, oily fish and fatty meat, such as bacon or sausages, and cheese.

- **Up to 6 months** for fruit, vegetables, nuts, cooked pulses, stocks, pestos, curry pastes, white fish and smaller cuts of meat and chicken.

- **Up to a year** for large joints of meat, whole chickens and egg whites.

Freezing Food Flat

- Pastry doughs, bags of minced meat, purées and sauces will all thaw more evenly and quickly if they are spread flat rather than clumped in a ball or cube. Try spreading food in a zip-lock bag, freezing on a tray, then slotting into its relevant place once frozen.

- Freezing pulses, berries, chopped fruit and loose vegetables on a tray, before tipping into a freezer bag or container to store, is useful if you want to use food by the handful rather than thaw an entire batch.

Thawing Food

Ideally, remove from the freezer and chill in the fridge the day before eating. If short of time, submerge a container in cold water, changing it every 30 minutes, or zap your dish in the microwave. Leaving food at warm room temperature, or in hot water, to thaw can be dangerous, potentially causing food poisoning.

Super-Useful Basics to Buy In

Peas, broad beans, edamame beans and the little bricks of **leaf spinach** mean that there are always some readily available greens for sides, soups, salads and sauces. These greens are flash-frozen immediately after picking so that they retain their nutrients.

Frozen berries are often much more economical than fresh and work just as well for smoothies and some puddings (such as Summer Pudding, page 144).

Puff pastry is a brilliant standby, ideal for sweet or savoury tarts. It's a perfect convenience ingredient since it's a labour of love to make from scratch. Roll the pastry as thin as you can, score a frame, bake blind, then layer with a hummus and roasted vegetables or simple 50/50 mix of mascarpone and yogurt, with a little caster sugar, topped with piles of fresh fruit.

Bread freezes well – it's worth slicing half your loaf and freezing it (page 142) if you regularly end up throwing bread out.

Pitta bread is very useful as you can thaw it in the toaster, fill it with goodies and have a meal in minutes.

It's also worth batch baking a few loaves at a time to save on time and energy. They will keep brilliantly for 2–3 months.

Corn tortillas make a brilliant quick-supper ingredient to serve with some homemade Baked Beans (page 39), roasted vegetables and grated cheese. They can be prized apart when still partially frozen before heating in a pan, and any leftover tortillas can be brushed with oil and baked in an oven preheated to 180°C/160°C fan/ gas 4 for 5–10 minutes until crisp – perfect for dips and salads.

Mushroom and Lentil Ragu

A good ragu (often known as a Bolognese sauce) has to be one of the most comforting and versatile dishes in any home cook's repertoire. This deeply savoury combination happens to be meat free and can be used with pasta and a myriad of other dishes.

Perfect for batch cooking, you can double up this recipe and freeze in meal-sized portions for busy days. Remove from the freezer and thaw in the fridge overnight.

SERVES 6–8 (DEPENDING ON YOUR END DISH)

2 tbsp olive oil
1 onion, diced
2 carrots, diced
1 celery stick, diced
300g (10½oz) portobello or chestnut mushrooms, diced
3 garlic cloves, crushed
250g (9oz) pumpkin or any squash, peeled and diced
100ml (3½fl oz) red or white wine
3 tbsp tomato purée
400g (14oz) can chopped tomatoes
800ml (1¾ pints) vegetable stock
200g (7oz) dried green lentils
2 bay leaves
1–2 tbsp Worcestershire sauce (vegan varieties are available)
About 1 tbsp sherry vinegar
Pinch of caster sugar (optional)
Salt

Heat the olive oil in your largest saucepan over a low heat and fry the onion, carrots and celery while you prepare your other ingredients. The vegetables need to soften and just begin to colour, which will take about 10 minutes, stirring occasionally.

Add the mushrooms and garlic, then increase the heat to medium. The pan will seem almost squeaky dry but, as you stir, the mushrooms will collapse and release plenty of moisture.

Stir in the pumpkin, a pinch of salt, the wine, the tomato purée, the chopped tomatoes and the stock. Add the lentils and bay leaves, cover with a lid and cook on a gentle simmer for about 45 minutes, adding a dash of water if the pan seems dry.

Once the lentils are tender, balance the flavour with Worcestershire sauce and vinegar, tasting and gradually adding until the ragu sings. You may want to add a little more salt and even a pinch of sugar, depending on the sweetness of your tomatoes.

COOKING FOR A RESOLUTE CARNIVORE? TRY THIS

Not everyone wants to ditch the meat in their diet; flexibility is key to winning over family members or friends who can't get their heads around the idea of enjoying vegetarian dishes. This ragu can be an opportunity to swap out a proportion of meat for the healthy, fibre-loaded lentils.

Just add 200g (7oz) minced beef or lamb instead of the mushrooms, stirring over a high heat and crumbling up the meat as you go. Once the meat has lost its raw appearance, add the remaining ingredients and continue as before.

Alternatively, replace the mushrooms with 200g (7oz) finely diced chorizo and fry until your pan turns a glorious shade of orange, then continue as before.

Changing It Up

Try adding diced celeriac or swede instead of squash for a distinctive wintery version.

For a bit of Iberian flavour, diced red pepper is fabulous added along with the initial onion, carrot and celery trio. Add 1 good tsp sweet smoked paprika and a pinch of dried thyme once your mushrooms have collapsed, stir-fry for 1 minute and continue as before.

Play around with the herbs:
- Finely chopped, fresh rosemary is perfect for Cottage Garden Pie (right), while dried oregano will give a more Italian vibe. Add these at the same time as the bay.

- A handful of basil or wild garlic leaves, ripped and stirred in just before serving, give a fabulous fresh punch.

Increase the savoury 'umami' depth by adding a leftover Parmesan rind at the same time as the pumpkin. It will infuse the sauce as it cooks, and you can scoop it out later.

Try adding about 20g (¾oz) soaked and chopped porcini mushrooms along with their soaking liquid.

Once cooked, divide your ragu in half and try adding a dash of full-fat milk, or 2 tbsp cream, to one half of it. Now you have two dishes; it's amazing how different they will taste.

WITH POACHED EGGS

SERVES 4

Heat half of the ragu in a saucepan and make 4 little wells in the surface, breaking an egg into each. Sprinkle over some freshly chopped chives, basil, chervil, parsley – whatever you have to hand. Add a pinch of salt and chilli flakes. Cover with a lid and cook over a medium heat for 3–5 minutes until the eggs are cooked to your liking. Perfect with brown rice and a blob of yogurt or just some good crusty bread.

COTTAGE GARDEN PIE

SERVES 4

Place half the cooked ragu in an ovenproof container and top with a layer of creamy mashed potato. Sprinkle with breadcrumbs and a splash of olive oil or a few nubs of butter. Either assemble hot and place under a hot grill until the top looks crunchy and golden OR if preparing ahead and cooking from cold, preheat the oven to 200°C/180°C fan/gas 6 and cook for about 30 minutes.

The Roasted Vegetable Centrepiece: Roasted Celeriac with Tomato and Lemon Sauce

A whole head of cauliflower, a celeriac, a large swede or an entire squash can make a dramatic centrepiece for a meal – something to carve with a bit of ceremony, showing that vegetables can be stars of the show too. Do make the most of your hot oven – roast beetroot, squash, peppers and aubergines at the same time to stow away for other meals.

Serve with some Steam-fried Greens (page 73) and a bowl of pulses, grains or both.

SERVES 4

1 medium celeriac (about 1kg/2lb 4oz)
3 tbsp extra-virgin olive oil
1 tsp coarse sea salt
Leaves from 2 sprigs of thyme
1 onion, diced
4 garlic cloves, crushed
2 x 400g (14oz) cans chopped tomatoes
Finely grated zest and juice of ½ lemon
100ml (3½fl oz) double cream, or 2 tbsp tahini
75g (2¾oz) Parmesan cheese (or 4 tbsp nutritional yeast)
100g (3½oz) roasted hazelnuts, roughly chopped
1 small bunch of parsley, finely chopped
1 small garlic clove, finely chopped
Salt and pepper

Preheat the oven to 200ºC/180ºC fan/gas 6.

Scrub the celeriac thoroughly, particularly around the tangled roots, then pat dry with a towel.

Place the celeriac on a large sheet of foil, rub in 1 tbsp of the olive oil and sprinkle with the salt and thyme leaves. Wrap up into a parcel and roast for 1½ hours. Carefully open up the foil and then roast for a further 45 minutes to caramelise and brown.

Meanwhile, make the sauce. Heat the remaining olive oil in a small pan over a low heat and fry the onion for 10 minutes, or until soft. Add the crushed garlic and, once you are hit by its intoxicating aroma, tip in the tomatoes. Simmer for about 20 minutes, then add the lemon juice and cream (or tahini for a dairy-free version). Season with salt and plenty of pepper.

Mix the lemon zest, Parmesan (or nutritional yeast), hazelnuts, parsley and chopped garlic together in a bowl.

Slice the whole celeriac into wedges at the table, serve with the tomato sauce and sprinkle with the nut mixture.

One-pan Cauliflower and Carlin Pea Curry

The beauty of this dish is that everything happens in one bowl and a large roasting tin. Broccoli, Tenderstem or romanesco can be swapped in for the cauliflower.

The Carlin peas have a fabulous nutty flavour but do use chickpeas if you can't find them. Adding a cooked pulse to the vegetable immediately makes this a substantial stand-alone meal, but you can always serve it with rice or flatbread too.

SERVES 4

1 medium cauliflower, broken into florets, green leaves cut into thick strips
1 red pepper, deseeded and cut into thick slices
3 tbsp vegetable oil, such as rapeseed or sunflower
2 garlic cloves, crushed
1 tbsp grated fresh root ginger
4 spring onions, sliced
2 tbsp medium curry powder
½ tsp salt
14 cherry tomatoes, halved
2 x 400g (14oz) cans Carlin peas or chickpeas, drained, or 500g (1lb 2oz) home-cooked
400ml (14fl oz) passata
1 small bunch of fresh coriander, roughly chopped
Juice of ½–1 lemon
100ml (3½fl oz) natural yogurt, to serve

Preheat the oven to 220°C/200°C fan/gas 7.

Toss the cauliflower florets and red pepper strips with half of the vegetable oil in a large bowl. Tip them into your largest roasting tin and place in the oven for 10–15 minutes.

Meanwhile, mix the chopped cauliflower leaves (and any sliced stalk), garlic, ginger, spring onions, curry powder, salt and remaining oil together in the original bowl.

Once the cauliflower has begun to brown add the curry mix to the roasting tin, turning the vegetables over in the oily spices with tongs. Add the tomatoes, cut-side up, and roast for a further 5 minutes.

Now mix the Carlin peas or chickpeas, the passata and half the coriander in the oily spice bowl. Tip into the roasting tin and cook for 5 minutes – just enough to heat the pulses through.

Squeeze over enough lemon juice to give a good tang, sprinkle with the remaining coriander and serve with a spoonful of yogurt.

HOW ABOUT?
- Replacing the curry powder with ras el hanout (a Moroccan spice blend) and adding a few green olives with the cherry tomatoes for a different spin. Serve with couscous.
- Replacing the curry powder with 1–2 tbsp of chipotle paste, 1 tsp dried oregano and 1 tsp ground cumin. Use black beans as your pulse, lime instead of lemon and serve with tortillas.

Mushroom and Tarragon Galette

Not only do mushrooms deliver big-time with their intense, savoury flavour, but they are also an extraordinarily water-efficient crop to grow. Cultivated mushrooms require little light and space too, and can be grown on potting compost made from recycled waste, and even spent coffee grounds. This mushroom filling would be fabulous on a slice of good, rustic toast if you don't have time to make the galette.

SERVES 6

Pastry
200g (7oz) wholegrain spelt, emmer or einkorn flour (or wholemeal plain flour)
Pinch of salt
Plenty of coarsely ground black pepper
100g (3½oz) cold butter, cubed
65g (2¼oz) full-fat crème fraîche
Tiny splash of cold water (optional)

Filling
500g (1lb 2oz) chestnut or cremini mushrooms
250g (9oz) shiitake or king oyster mushrooms
2 tbsp rapeseed oil
20g (¾oz) butter
1 garlic clove, finely chopped
1 tbsp grainy mustard
4 sprigs of tarragon, leaves removed and chopped
100g (3½oz) full-fat crème fraîche
30g (1oz) fresh breadcrumbs
75g (2¾oz) walnuts, roughly chopped
Salt and pepper

Warm garlic butter
50g (1¾oz) butter
1 garlic clove, finely chopped
A small handful of fresh parsley, chives and a few bits of tarragon
Squeeze of lemon juice
Salt and pepper

To make the pastry, mix the flour, salt and pepper together in a large bowl, then add the cold butter. Using a table knife or pastry scraper, cut and stir the butter for 2 minutes, tossing the cubes around in the flour, then rub the butter into the flour using your fingertips until the mixture looks like rough breadcrumbs. Add the crème fraîche and stir it through with the table knife or pastry scraper. Gather the dough together into a ball in your hands, adding a tiny splash of cold water if it feels too dry.

Roll the pastry out into a disc about 30cm (12 inches) in diameter between two sheets of baking paper (these can be reused), then leave to chill in the fridge while you prepare the filling.

For the filling, slice the chestnut or cremini mushrooms into thick slices. If using shiitake mushrooms, remove the stalks and chop these finely but leave the mushrooms whole. If using king oyster mushrooms, cut them in half lengthways.

Heat the oil in your largest frying pan (or you may need two pans) and fry the mushrooms, stirring occasionally until the mushrooms have browned and begun to collapse and lose their moisture. Toss in the butter and garlic and stir until it's aromatic. Add the mustard, tarragon and crème fraîche and cook to reduce away any excess moisture. Season with plenty of salt and pepper to taste. Set aside to cool.

Preheat the oven to 190°C/170°C fan/gas 5.

Place the pastry on its paper on a large, flat baking tray and remove the top sheet of paper. Sprinkle the pastry with the breadcrumbs and walnuts, then spoon over the mushrooms, leaving a 4cm (1½-inch) margin around the edge. Carefully fold the pastry around the margin up and over some of the filling, leaving most of it exposed. Don't worry if it cracks slightly; it's meant to look rustic. Bake in the oven for 30 minutes, or until the pastry is golden.

Meanwhile, melt the butter in small pan, add the garlic and cook until the garlic releases its aroma. Add the herbs and season with salt, pepper and a squeeze of lemon juice to taste.

Serve hot or at room temperature, drizzled with the warm garlic butter.

TRY THIS

Replace the garlic butter with some grated cheese; 50g (1¾oz) Gruyère would be fantastic, but it could be some random heels of cheese from the fridge. Just add the grated cheese over the galette before it goes into the oven.

Not a fan of tarragon? Lemon thyme would work well here.

This spelt pastry case is fabulously versatile – try filling your galette with:
- Roasted beetroot and onions (page 22) and a little goat's cheese.
- Smoky peppers and aubergines (page 130) with cannellini and pesto 'hummus' (page 41) to serve.
- Roasted squash, onion, rosemary and feta.

Always sprinkle the pastry surface with breadcrumbs before adding the filling to soak up any excess moisture. Adding nuts to the filling is a good plan for some extra texture.

Roast Squash and Black bean Tacos

Good-quality corn tortillas are a fabulous freezer standby as they are wholegrain, add great texture and are an incredibly versatile vehicle for all sorts of leftovers. When roasting squash for this recipe, it's worth roasting an extra tray; this makes use of the oven space and gives you the base of a lunchbox salad for the following day.

SERVES 4

- 1–1.5kg (2lb 4oz–3lb 5oz) firm-fleshed squash, such as Crown Prince, Carnival or Red Kuri
- 3 tbsp rapeseed oil
- 2 x 400g (14oz) cans black beans, drained
- 1 tsp dried oregano
- 1 tbsp cumin seeds
- 2 garlic cloves, crushed
- 2 tsp chipotle purée or paste or chipotles en adobo (chop any whole peppers), or more to taste
- 2 limes
- 200ml (7fl oz) soured cream or Greek-style yogurt
- 12–16 corn tortillas, depending on size
- 100g (3½oz) cheese, such as Cheddar, Cheshire, Lancashire or feta, grated or crumbled
- Pink Onion Pickle (page 47)
- A large handful of coriander, leaves picked
- Salt

Preheat the oven to 200°C/180°C fan/gas 6.

Chop the squash in half, spoon out the seeds and set aside, then cut the squash into about 16 segments. If you can push your thumbnail through the raw skin it will be perfectly good to eat and add some wonderful texture to the dish. Toss the squash around in 2 tbsp of the oil and a generous pinch of salt on two large baking trays. The squash needs plenty of space so that it roasts rather than stews. Roast in the oven for about 20 minutes before flipping the squash over to caramelise for a further 15–20 minutes.

Wash the reserved squash seeds, removing any pulp, then dry them before adding to the squash slices for the last 15 minutes of the roasting time.

Meanwhile, place the black beans in a large bowl with the remaining oil, the oregano, cumin, garlic and a good pinch of salt and stir. Add 2 tsp of the chipotle purée or chipotle in adobo and stir through, then taste and add more if it is missing the kick you're after.

Tip all the squash onto one tray and use the other tray for your beans – they'll only require about 5 minutes to warm through in the oven.

Finely grate the lime zest and add along with the juice of 1 lime to the soured cream or yogurt in a bowl. Cut the remaining lime into quarters and set aside.

Heat a heavy frying pan and toast the corn tortillas for 2 minutes on each side until warmed through with the odd brown speckle. Wrap in a warm tea towel until ready to serve.

It's fun to assemble your own tacos, so place the roasted squash and seeds, the beans, cheese, soured cream, pickled onions and coriander on the table with the basket of cloth-wrapped tacos alongside.

NO TORTILLAS?
The squash and all the trimmings would be delicious with brown rice or quinoa as a base.

Seeking Out More Sustainable Fish

Fresh fish in crisp batter, eaten straight from the paper or box, is a national institution – but for how much longer? That old expression 'there are plenty more fish in the sea' no longer rings true. In fact, 90 per cent of global fish stocks are either overfished or at risk of being overfished, according to the UN (United Nations). There's no question; we must change the way we buy and eat fish if our fragile ocean ecosystems are to survive.

Eating much less fish is one obvious and effective answer to the situation, and there's no doubt that a shift towards more plant-focused diets is as vital for our seas as it is for the land. Thankfully, there are also ways that we can make a difference if, and when, we do decide to enjoy fish.

The world of aquaculture is developing fast, with many innovative and increasingly sustainable methods being put into practice. Fish feeds with a high ratio of plant and/or insect protein (rather than purely wild fish) have been developed, and ways to reduce antibiotic use and preserve natural habitats are also emerging. Farmed fish could become one of the most efficient ways to produce the animal protein of the future. Salmon, sea bass, sea bream, tilapia and prawns are among the most commonly available farmed fish; seek out those with ASC (Aquaculture Stewardship Council) accreditation, guaranteeing environmentally and socially responsible seafood.

In the UK, our appetite for the handful known as **'the big five'** is almost insatiable; sales of salmon, prawns, cod, haddock and tuna far outstrip those of all the other fish on offer put together. These stocks are under severe pressure, leading to often damaging, intensive farming practices in the case of salmon and warm-water prawns, and overfishing of cod, haddock and tuna.

It's about making informed choices. Cornish hake can be a great alternative at the fish and chip shop, while you could decide to serve local

mackerel at your summer barbecue rather than tuna. Pollack, gurnard, megrim and dab have been overlooked in the past and yet they offer so much in texture and flavour, and are often well priced.

Getting to know a good fishmonger who values provenance, as well as freshness, is the surest way to buy fish from the smaller boats that support our coastal communities and use more sustainable fishing methods. These day-boats are not so focused on one species of fish, unlike many of the industrial trawlers that often throw by-catch (unintentionally netted fish) back into the sea. Look out, or ask, for fishing methods such as pole- or hand-line-caught, or, when it comes to shellfish, hand-dived rather than dredged. Many areas no longer have a local fishmonger and, if this is the case, it may be worth ordering online from a reliable source that delivers to your area.

Check out the (MSC) Marine Stewardship Council online for their ratings on making better wild fish choices when it comes to levels of fish stocks, their locations and the way they are fished. You can also look for the MSC blue labels in fishmongers and supermarkets, indicating that your choice of fish is more sustainable. Also, try the Marine Conservation Society's Good Fish Guide app.

Super-simple Fish Stew

Preserved Fish Can Reduce Food Waste

Seafood is highly perishable, leading to well over a quarter of the catch being discarded after landing. We're pushing fish stocks towards extinction, throwing so much precious fish away simply because we don't eat it in time.

Frozen fish is a good plan if you don't have a regular fish supplier: most fish will have been flash-frozen when super fresh, a world away from the gluey-looking specimens lurking on some fish counters. Frozen fish tends to be cheaper and will keep well for about 2 months.

Smoking is another option, extending the life of the fish so that we're less likely to waste it. Just one fillet of mackerel or trout, or a few slices of smoked salmon, can flavour an entire platter of salad if you're making your fish stretch that bit further.

Quality canned fish is enjoying new levels of interest in Britain; at last we are beginning to understand the Spanish and Portuguese fondness for it. Essentially, it's about recognising canned seafood as a different ingredient rather than a second-rate cousin of fresh. Fish can be processed in peak condition at the height of its season and this reduces wastage. A few anchovies can add the umami magic that lifts an entire dish, while a can of sardines makes the ultimate high tea, served grilled on a piece of toast.

SERVES 4

It's worth remembering that the best advice when shopping for fish is to look for the freshest, most sustainable fish on the day. Look for bright eyes, vibrant gills, shiny skin and firm flesh. If in doubt, smell it, and, above all, take advice from a supplier that you trust.

A simple recipe that doesn't call for any specific type of fish is quite useful to have in your repertoire, making the most of what's best on the day. Use any white-fleshed fish for this one.

Chop 2 small waxy potatoes per person into bite-sized pieces. Add these to a large saucepan with a good splash of olive oil and fry while you dice an onion. Add the onion and 2–3 crushed garlic cloves. Stir and add some fresh thyme, parsley or basil and a finely sliced bulb of fennel.

Cover everything with water or fish stock (page 102), add the lid and boil for 10 minutes. Add 150ml (5fl oz) white wine, a good squeeze of tomato purée and salt and pepper or chilli flakes.

Once the potatoes are just cooked through, add 120g (4oz) filleted, skinned and seasoned white fish per person (freeze any skin and bones for your next stock). Don't cut it into small pieces. Cover and simmer for 3–5 minutes until the fish has turned opaque. Serve with a squeeze of lemon, bread and maybe some garlicky mayonnaise.

Of course you could:

- Add 2 finely chopped carrots and celery sticks along with the onion.
- Use cooked butter beans instead of potato (just add at the same time as the wine).
- Add a pinch of saffron threads in with the herbs.
- Add 3–4 live mussels per person to steam on the top when you simmer the fish.

Mussel Power

Bivalves, such as mussels, oysters and clams, could offer us one of the best solutions of all when it comes to eating sustainably farmed seafood.

While much of global aquaculture relies on vast quantities of wild fish being caught to produce fish feed, bivalves require no feeding at all. They're filter feeders, living on microscopic organic matter in the water. In fact, these hinge-shelled molluscs actually clean the water, helping to reduce the excessive algal growth which has devastated marine life in many areas of the world.

Growing mussels on ropes can repair marine habitats too (which have been previously damaged by dredging and overfishing), supporting a vast biodiversity of creatures, from shrimp to crab, pollack to wrasse. It's just a question of providing the ropes for the mussels to grow on, redistributing the young from time to time, with no need for pesticides or antibiotics. It is low-intervention farming when compared with not just fish farming, but also animal and arable farming on land.

In Britain, mussels are the most widely available and economical shellfish, although we still eat relatively few compared to our European neighbours. It's time to dive in, as exports have fallen with post-Brexit trading regulations and mussel farmers could do with our support.

Mussels even shine on the nutritional side too, being high in protein and loaded with iron, selenium, zinc and the crucial omega-3 fatty acids that are so important for brain function and heart health.

Wild mussels can be fabulous when harvested sustainably. Do take care if foraging for mussels yourself – the water must not be polluted, otherwise all that filter feeding can lead to a dangerous build-up of toxins.

Preparing a batch of mussels when you get them home from the shops is very straightforward. Here's how:

Open the bag of mussels into a large bowl, cover with a damp cloth (as they need to breathe) and store in the fridge.

Before cooking (this can be a few hours ahead), cover the mussels with cold water and rattle them around the bowl with your hands. Most of the shells will close immediately. Tap any open mussels on the side of the bowl; if they still remain open they are probably dead, so discard them. The problem with dead mussels is that we have no idea how long ago they died, and mussel flesh can spoil very quickly and potentially cause food poisoning. Mussels with broken shells should be discarded too.

Pull any fibrous beards off the mussels and, if they are covered in barnacles or weed, scrub them thoroughly. One advantage of farmed mussels is that the shells will be cleaner and the mussels unlikely to be gritty as they are growing on ropes above the sandy ocean floor.

Your mussels are now ready to go. Cook immediately or keep in the fridge for a few hours until ready to use. Any mussels that open in the meantime are not a problem.

3 Ways with Mussels

MOULES MARINIÈRES

A classic, and the simplest way to cook mussels. Best enjoyed with a crusty baguette.

SERVES 4

- 2 shallots, finely diced
- 2 garlic cloves, finely chopped
- 50g (1¾oz) butter
- 2 bay leaves
- 6 sprigs of thyme
- 3 tbsp roughly chopped fresh parsley
- 150ml (5fl oz) dry white wine
- 1.75kg (3lb 13oz) live mussels, cleaned (page 171)
- Salt and pepper

Fry the shallots and garlic gently in the butter in a medium saucepan for about 5 minutes before adding the bay leaves, thyme and half of the parsley. Add a splash of the wine, bring to the boil, then set aside until your mussels are ready.

Pour the remaining wine into a wide pan large enough to hold all your mussels, and bring to the boil. Add the mussels and cover with a well-fitting lid. Cook for 4 minutes, or until the mussels have opened, shaking the pan a couple of times.

Mussels are readily available, environmentally sustainable, packed with nutrients and easy to cook. What's not to like? It's not often that something with such fabulous green credentials can seem so indulgent.

Given that grit can be a problem when cooking clams and mussels, a foolproof method is to steam the bivalves with the wine or cider in a separate pan from the sauce base, with the added benefit that all the sauce work can be done ahead of time.

If any mussels remain closed after cooking you may choose to discard them as they could still be a little raw.

Scoop the mussels into a large serving bowl. Now slowly tip their cooking liquor into the sauce base, leaving behind any sand or grit that has settled at the bottom of the mussel pan. Stir the sauce over a high heat until piping hot. Season with salt and pepper and pour over the mussels. Sprinkle with the remaining parsley and serve immediately.

TRY adding a pinch of saffron along with 3 tbsp double cream instead of the bay and thyme. You'll have a perfect pasta sauce that's especially good with linguine.

MUSSELS WITH CHORIZO AND CIDER

A 'surf-and-turf' combination from northern Spain where, similar to our British apple-growing regions, cider is king.

SERVES 4

- 200g (7oz) chorizo, finely diced
- 3 medium leeks, finely sliced
- 2 tbsp olive oil
- 2 garlic cloves, finely chopped
- 1 small sprig of thyme
- 150ml (5fl oz) dry cider
- 1.75kg (3lb 13oz) live mussels, cleaned (page 171)
- 3 tbsp roughly chopped fresh flat-leaf parsley
- Salt and pepper

Fry the chorizo and leeks in the olive oil in a large frying pan for about 10 minutes. Add the garlic and thyme, stirring until you smell the wafts of garlic. Now add a small splash of the cider to calm the pan and set aside.

Pour the remaining cider into a wide pan large enough to hold all your mussels, and bring to the boil. Add the mussels and cover with a well-fitting lid. Cook for 4 minutes, or until the mussels have opened, shaking the pan a couple of times.

Scoop the cooked mussels into a serving bowl. Now slowly tip their cooking liquor into the chorizo and leeks, leaving behind any sand or grit that has settled at the bottom of the mussel pan. Taste and season, before bringing to the boil and tipping over the mussels. Sprinkle with parsley and serve.

TRY serving with 400g (14oz) cooked butter beans for a more substantial dish; just add the beans to the chorizo and leek mixture at the same time as the cider.

CREAMY CURRIED MUSSELS

Traditionally served with bread in France, this dish, known as *mouclade*, is also great with rice if you're wanting to make a meal of your mussels.

SERVES 4

- 2 shallots, finely diced
- 2 garlic cloves, finely chopped
- 1 lemongrass stalk, chopped
- 25g (1oz) butter
- 1 tsp medium curry powder
- ½ tsp celery salt
- 100ml (3½fl oz) double cream
- 3 tbsp fresh chopped coriander
- 150ml (5fl oz) white wine
- 1.75kg (3lb 13oz) live mussels, cleaned (page 171)
- Juice of ½ lemon
- 1 red chilli, finely sliced (optional)
- Pepper

Fry the shallots, garlic and lemongrass in the butter in a medium saucepan for about 5 minutes before adding the curry powder and celery salt. Stir until you can really smell the spices, then add the cream and half the coriander. Bring to the boil, then set aside.

Pour the wine into a wide pan large enough to hold all your mussels and bring to the boil. Add the mussels and cover with a well-fitting lid. Cook for 4 minutes, or until the mussels have opened, shaking the pan a couple of times.

Scoop your mussels into a large bowl or individual servings. Now slowly tip their cooking liquor into the curry sauce, leaving behind any sand or grit that has settled at the bottom of the mussel pan. Heat the sauce until piping hot and season with lemon juice and pepper to taste. Pour over the mussels, sprinkle with the remaining coriander and the chilli (if using) and serve.

Plum and Almond Upside Down Cake

This is a wonderful sweet treat to finish a meal. It's one base recipe, one tin and you have a cake for all seasons using whatever fruit is at its best.

SERVES 8

Butter or oil, for greasing
20g (¾oz) butter, diced
3 tbsp light muscovado sugar
8–10 ripe plums, halved and stoned
1 tbsp toasted flaked almonds, for sprinkling
cream, mascarpone or yogurt, to serve (optional)

Cake batter
125g (4½oz) plain flour (or a mix of 50/50 wholemeal and plain)
2 tsp baking powder
50g (1¾oz) ground almonds
150g (5oz) butter, fully softened and diced
150g (5oz) light muscovado sugar
3 medium eggs, beaten
2 tbsp milk (plant-based or dairy)
1 tsp vanilla extract

Preheat the oven to 170°C/150°C fan/gas 3. Grease a 23cm (9 inch) springform cake tin and line the base with baking paper. Place the cake tin on a baking tray.

Scatter the diced butter over the base of the tin and warm through in the oven until melted. Swirl the tin so that the melted butter covers the base, then sprinkle over the sugar. Arrange the plums, skin-side up, over the bottom of the tin.

Sift the flour and baking powder together into a large bowl, then add all the remaining cake batter ingredients and whisk for 2 minutes until well combined.

Spread the cake batter carefully over the fruit and bake in the oven for 50 minutes, or until golden brown and a skewer inserted into the middle comes out clean.

Leave to cool on a wire rack for about 10 minutes before running a knife around the cake to loosen. Invert the cake onto a serving plate, unclip the tin, then remove the paper carefully from the top. Some particularly juicy fruit oozes so much moisture that the top of the cake may look a little soft. If this is the case, brown for a couple of minutes under the grill.

Sprinkle over the flaked almonds and serve warm, or at room temperature, with cream, mascarpone or yogurt if you fancy.

TRY THIS
Try swapping in these options instead of the plums and vanilla extract:

3–4 apples, quartered + a handful of blackberries + 1 tsp ground cinnamon.

3–4 pears, peeled and quartered + 100g (3½oz) chocolate chips, folded in at the last minute.

6–8 apricots, halved and stoned + 1 tsp whole cardamom seeds, bruised.

400g (14oz) rhubarb, cut in 5cm (2 inch) pieces + 1 tsp dried ginger + 3 knobs stem ginger, diced.

THE
GREEN
KITCHEN

Saving Energy (and Money) in the Kitchen

The only compensation for the rising energy bills hitting our household budgets is perhaps that we're more focused on reducing our consumption, cutting down on emissions in our bid to cut costs.

In General

If you are looking at investing in a new hob any time soon then induction, using magnetic currents to produce heat, is by far the most efficient way of cooking your food, even beating a kettle when it comes to boiling water.

How many times do we boil the kettle every day? Heating up just the water we require each time can cut the energy usage by up to half.

Putting a lid on a pan when boiling, and even simmering, liquids conserves energy every time.

Slow cookers can be an easy and extraordinarily economical way to make stews, ragus and curries, using scarcely more energy than a light bulb and so much less energy than putting a pot in the oven. Look out for new models where you can use the inner pan on your hob to sear or boil, and then continue cooking in the slow cooker – so much less faff and washing up.

Pressure cookers are an absolute win-win for both time and energy, dramatically reducing cooking times. Once mastered (and it's not complicated), pressure cooking makes preparing pulses, grains and tougher cuts of meat a cinch. Modern models are foolproof too, blowing all those tales of Great-aunt Edith's exploding chicken casserole out of the water.

Batch Cooking

- Cooking a large pot of pulses or grains as the bedrock of dishes to last a few days makes sense as far as energy consumption (and your own time) goes.
- Think beyond tonight's meal when, for instance, making soups; doubling up the base recipe before adding the stock can give you a vegetable purée for the following day or a stack of baby food to freeze in small containers (silicone mini muffin trays are perfect).
- It's useful to prepare numerous portions of slow-cooked dishes such as stews, ragus, curries and sauces. Be sure to cool them fully before refrigerating or freezing, otherwise your chiller will have to work harder.

Making Full Use of Cooking Heat

Consider using steaming pans that stack one above the other, using just one hob to cook two or three different vegetables in one go. If you are using the oven, be sure to utilise all the space – there's never an excuse for an empty shelf.

- Slipping a tray of vegetables in to roast takes no time at all and they will always come in handy for salads, dips and sandwiches.
- Bring an ovenproof pan of pulses or grains to the boil on the hob, then continue cooking in the oven.
- Stock can be bubbling away, working its magic, quietly in the oven.

A Few Eco Cleaning Hacks

We can tread more lightly on the planet not just by choosing to eat more mindfully, but also with all the other products we buy, use and consume in life. In choosing our household cleaning products, we often forget that everything we pour down the drain ends up in our waterways, and eventually the sea – and we're also often needlessly breathing noxious fumes.

For now, let's focus on the kitchen, but once you've discovered how easy, cheap and satisfying it is to use homemade cleaning products you'll probably reassess what you use in the rest of the house too. The vast range of cleaning agents on offer persuade us that we need a specific product for every job around the house, resulting in cupboards of endless plastic containers and dozens of harmful chemicals.

Bicarbonate of soda and white vinegar will do almost every job you can imagine. Try to buy in bulk; many zero waste stores stock them so you can refill your containers, but otherwise find suppliers online (buying smaller packs designed for cooking will be very expensive).

Bicarbonate of Soda

- Keep a small open tub of bicarbonate of soda in your fridge to absorb odours.

- Sprinkle into the bottom of your rubbish bin under the bin bag to keep it fresh.

- Put 2 tbsp bicarbonate of soda into a stained saucepan (who hasn't boiled their beans dry at least once?), cover with water and bring to the boil. Switch off the heat and leave to cool before brushing the pan clean.

- To remove sticky labels from jars, mix together a paste of 50/50 bicarbonate of soda and vegetable oil. Smooth the paste over the sticky residue on the jar and leave for 30 minutes. Rub off with a cloth and wash in soapy water.

White Vinegar (Also Known as Spirit Vinegar)

A blend of 50/50 white vinegar and water will be perfect for cleaning inside the fridge, the hob, work surfaces, windows and floors. Just mix in a recycled cleaning spray bottle and you're off (don't use on marble or treated hardwood as it may stain).

If you're not keen on the sharp smell of vinegar then you can add leftover citrus peels. Either add some citrus peel to cold vinegar and leave it for at least a week, or heat the vinegar until it's nearly boiling and then pour it over a jar of lemon, lime or orange peels (no fruit, or the mixture will become sticky and cloudy) and leave for a couple of days. Strain the vinegar through a fine sieve or muslin cloth and mix with an equal quantity of water. You can also try adding eucalyptus leaves or sprigs of rosemary, thyme or mint. Alternatively, you can add a couple of drops of essential oil to your vinegar and shake well before using. But be aware that some essential oils are bad or potentially toxic for pets.

Cleaning the Oven

Make a paste of equal parts bicarbonate of soda to water, spread over the inside of the oven, avoiding elements, and leave to work overnight. The next day, wipe off with a damp cloth or scrape off carefully if the dirt is stubborn. Don't use an abrasive. Spray with white vinegar to remove any residue and finally wipe off with a damp cloth.

Less Packaging

It's good to have a store of reusable tote bags by your front door, in your car and in your handbag (the recycled polyester bags fold down very small) so you can always avoid picking up a plastic carrier bag. Do keep in mind that cotton and recycled polyester bags are only sustainable options if we use them over and over again.

Zero waste stores are leading the way when it comes to refilling existing jars and containers with essential food and household items, but we need to make this the norm for everyone, everywhere. If you don't have access to, or the opportunity to visit, a refill store, then it's time to ask your supermarket manager when they will be offering unpackaged options. Initially it may seem like an extra hassle taking your empty containers with you when you go shopping, but soon enough it will become a habit.

Buy loose fruit and vegetables whenever you can, sending a message to our suppliers and shopkeepers that we don't want, or need, all the plastic packaging.

Jam jars, bean jars and other food containers can be reused again and again for storing leftover marinades, sauces, pestos and dressings (see Freezer Tips on page 156), reducing the use of zip-lock bags, plastic containers and cling film.

Rather than covering bowls with cling film, try using a plate or a reusable wax wrap. If you are considering buying food storage containers then glass versions with plastic fitted lids are a boon for leftovers; they can go straight into the freezer, minus the lid, in the same container.

At some point we have to recognise that convenience is not the priority: our planet matters more. The first, most vital step, is reducing our need for single-use packaging – and particularly plastic. Then it's a case of recycling everything that we possibly can.

More Recycling

Right now in the UK over 14 million tonnes of rubbish are sent to landfill every year, which accounts for about 55 per cent of our household waste. We need to turn things around. Washing and sorting our recyclable waste is something we can all do. Every one of us can make a difference.

Did You Know?

It takes the same amount of energy to make one new aluminium can as it does to recycle 20. Aluminium can be successfully recycled numerous times and yet millions of cans are sent to UK landfill every day.

We make and use 20 times more plastic today than we did 50 years ago. Despite the fact that plastic in landfill will take up to 500 years to decompose, as a country we are still recycling under half of our plastic.

Glass is 100 per cent recyclable and yet we currently only recycle about half of it. Countries such as Finland and Switzerland recycle about 90 per cent of their glass.

Milk bottles made from low-density polyethylene are highly recyclable; rinse, crush and replace the lid before adding to your household recycling. Plant milks (page 81) tend to come in Tetra Pak cartons; rinse and crush these before taking them to a suitable recycling point (or check if your kerbside collection will accept them).

Every Step You Take,
Every Move You Make

It's not about changing everything at once, and it's not about being perfect; it's about every one of us doing what we can.

There are so many ways to reconnect with our food, eating in a way that brings us joy and good health, while respecting the world around us. Hopefully, *A Good Appetite* will galvanise you into action; but this isn't a diet or a quick fix, it's a journey. And, if you need a little kick-start to set you on your way, here are a few ideas:

1 How about introducing a new 'whole food' into your diet each week? That can be any new fruit, vegetable, grain, pulse, nut or seed that you don't usually buy – just basically a whole, natural food that nobody has messed around with.

2 Keep a waste log for a few weeks. Count how many pieces of plastic, glass and cardboard are in the recycling and try to reduce week on week. Once you've found a new, packaging-free source for a product, you've done the hard work; try to go back there and in no time it will become habit.

3 Try the '30 different plant foods in a week' challenge, chalking up your tally on a blackboard or a keeping a list on the fridge. Make a slaw or a minestrone, add fresh fruit to your granola, sprinkle toasted seeds on salads, add fresh herbs to your pasta: it's all about variety.

4 Take some time to connect with your local food scene. Shopping doesn't have to be a dreaded chore; seeking out food from a specialist shop, a local market, a farm store or a community garden can be a wonderfully positive way to spend downtime. Even if you're in the middle of a city, or out in the wilds, there are plenty of wonderful small suppliers to connect with online.

5 Grow at least one thing; even if you're short of time or space, a few pots of herbs on the windowsill will save you money, enhance your cooking and lift your spirits.

6 If you have children in the house try cooking together for at least one meal a week. Kids who get involved in the kitchen are usually more adventurous and less likely to waste food.

7 Eat together whenever you can. If your household has got into the habit of eating at different times in separate spaces then try to have more meals together. Gradual change is probably best – otherwise the new regime will feel like a crackdown, and you may have a revolt on your hands. Some days will be impossible, with everyone on different agendas and timetables, in any case, but taking time to share the table is vital for our relationships with both food and one another.

Resources

SHOPPING
Zero waste stores: you can find your closest at thezerowastenetwork.com

A COUPLE OF WONDERFUL WEBSITES FOR DRY GOODS
For British-grown pulses, grains and seeds:
hodmedods.co.uk
For spices steenbergs.co.uk

ORGANIC VEG & MEAT BOXES
Both local and countrywide:
soilassociation.org 'find a box scheme'
pastureforlife.org

A SEASONAL FOOD GUIDE
nationaltrust.org.uk/discover/gardening-tips/
guide-to-seasonal-food

FORAGING
wildfooduk.com
britishlocalfood.com
nationaltrust.org.uk/visit/countryside-
woodland/places-to-forage-for-wild-garlic
nationaltrust.org.uk/discover/nature/trees-
plants/blackberry-picking-tips

TIPS ON BUYING MORE SUSTAINABLE FISH
mcsuk.org/goodfishguide

ENCOURAGING CHILDREN TO EAT MORE FRUIT AND VEGETABLES
tasteeducation.com

WASTE AND RECYCLING
Food waste
lovefoodhatewaste.com

Useful apps
toogoodtogo.co.uk
olioex.com

PLASTIC POLLUTION
citytosea.org.uk and their refill app and water map app when travelling abroad

RECYCLING
recyclenow.com
walesrecycles.org.uk
zerowastescotland.org.uk

FOOD AND FARMING CHARITIES AND SOCIAL ENTERPRISES
* eating-better.org
* fairtrade.org.uk
* landworkersalliance.org.uk
* planetbaseddiets.panda.org (WWF)
* soilassociation.org
* sustainablefoodtrust.org
* sustainweb.org

SOME FASCINATING AND INFORMATIVE BOOKS
* Balz, M., *No-Waste Composting*, Cool Springs Press (2021)
* Gilmartin, Dr C., *Fermented Foods: A Practical Guide*, The Crowood Press Ltd (2020)
* Knight, L., *Forage: Wild plants to Gather, Cook and Eat*, Laurence King Publishing (2021)
* Pollan, M., *The Omnivore's Dilemma*, Large Print Press (2007)
* Rebanks, J., *English Pastoral: An Inheritance*, Penguin Books (2021)
* Spector, T., *Spoon-Fed*, Vintage (2020)
* Steel, C., *Sitopia: How Food Can Save the World*, Vintage (2021)
* Wilson B., *The Way We Eat Now*, Fourth Estate (new edition, 2020)

Index

Note: page numbers in **bold** refer to illustrations.

A

acidity 15, 64
alcohol intake 137
almond 139
    nectarine, raspberry, thyme
        and toasted almonds 147
    plum and almond upside-down
        cake 174, **175**
almond milk 81
aluminium cans 180
anchovy 14, 79, 139, 169
animal welfare 76, 81
anxiety 108
appetite 7, 119–20
apple 29, 74, 99, 149–50
    local apple platter 147
    smoked quinoa, kale and apple
        salad 30, **31**
aquaculture 168, 171
Aquaculture Stewardship Council
    (ASC) 168
artichoke, Jerusalem artichoke
    soup 60, **61**
asparagus 104
    socca with asparagus and
        creamed cannellini 112, **113**
aubergine
    babaganoush 131
    smoky peppers and aubergines
        130–1
    zaalouk 131
autumn 153–75

B

babaganoush (Middle Eastern
    aubergine dip) 131
bacon 64, 104, 156
bacteria 48–9, 80, 107, 136
    see also gut microbiome
bags, reusable 179
banana 54
    banana, cardamom and dark
        chocolate bites 116, **117**

banana ice cream 154
barley flakes 24
basil 92, 139, 143
batch cooking 155, 178
bean(s) 37, 67, 79, 157
    baked beans **38**, 39
    bean burgers 129
    Greek beans 39
    Italian beans 39
    Tex-Mex beans 39
    see also black bean; broad
        bean; butter bean; cannellini
        bean
beef 76, 77
    beef stock 102
    'eke out the meat' beef stew
        78, 79
    mushroom and lentil ragu 158
beetroot 29, 74
    beetroot tops 71
    butter bean and beetroot
        hummus 41
    roasted beetroot, pot barley
        and warm fava 'hummus' 22,
        23
    vegetable peeling crisps 70
berries 89, 147
    berry and flaxseed jam **32**, 33
    frozen 157
    and seasonal eating 58
    summer pudding 144
    see also blackberry
'best before' dates 53
bicarbonate of soda, as cleaning
    agent 179
biodiversity 26, 34–5, 76–7,
    108, 171
black bean 37
    roast squash and black bean
        tacos 166, **167**
    smoky black bean and peanut
        hummus 41
blackberry 8, 33, 89, 144, 149,
    154, 174
'bliss point' 20
blood sugar levels 134, 146

borlotti bean 37, 67
bran 20, 21
brassica stalks 70
bread
    spelt loaf 25
    flatbreads 128
    frozen 157
    panzanella salad 143
    stale 142–4
    summer pudding 144
    wasted 142–4
breadcrumbs 99, 129, 131, 142,
    164–5
brine 48–9
broad bean 70, 104, 157
broccoli 70, 103, 163
brodo, Italian-style 103
Brussels sprout 74, 100
bubble and squeak 97, 100, **101**
buckwheat 27, 35, 67, 103
    buckwheat pancakes 29
bulgur wheat 139
burgers, bean 129
butter 14
    warm garlic butter 164–5
butter bean 37
    bulgur, butter bean and
        summer greens salad with
        salsa verde **138**, 139
    butter bean and beetroot
        hummus 41

C

cabbage
    bubble and squeak 100
    cabbage and Parmesan slaw 74
    rainbow slaw 74, **75**
    steam-fried greens **72**, 73
    see also red cabbage
caffeine 137
cake, plum and almond upside
    down 174, **175**
camelina seed 17, 27, 99, 129
cancer 134
    bowel 20
canned foods 36, 169

cannellini bean 37
  baked beans **38**, 39
  cannellini bean and pesto
    hummus 41
  socca with asparagus and
    creamed cannellini 112, **113**
capers 15, 22, 139
carbon emissions 5, 76, 149
cardamom 16, 24, 46, 51, 147,
  154, 174
  banana, cardamom and dark
    chocolate bites 116, **117**
Carlin pea, one-pan cauliflower
  and Carlin pea curry **162**, 163
carrot 67, 79, 98, 158–9
  carrot and ginger soup 63
  carrot tops 71, 92
  spiced carrot or cauliflower
    pickle 47
  vegetable peeling crisps 70
cattle 76–7, 81
cauliflower 74
  one-pan cauliflower and Carlin
    pea curry **162**, 163
  spiced carrot or cauliflower
    pickle 47
celeriac 71, 74, 159
  celeriac and hazelnut soup 63
  celeriac tops 92
  roasted celeriac with tomato
    and lemon sauce 160, **161**
celery 30, 70–1, 79, 92
  Jerusalem artichoke soup 60
  minestrone 67
  mushroom and lentil ragu
    158–9
  roast chicken 98
  stuffing balls 99
chard 67, 100
cheese 80, 92, 135
  bean burgers 129
  homemade 'ricotta' 80
  leek and pumpkin speltotto
    with crumbled blue cheese
    82, **83**
  pears with sheep's cheese and

  honey 147
  roast squash and black bean
    tacos 166
  seasonality 59
  smoked quinoa, kale and apple
    salad 30
  vegetable fritters 126
  warm lentil salad with roasted
    radish, whipped cheese and
    wild garlic chimichurri 94, **95**
  see also feta; Parmesan
chia seed 17, 27, 99, 129
chicken 76
  Asian chicken noodle soup 103
  chicken stock 102–3
  roast chicken **96**, 97, 98
chickpea
  chocolate, chickpea and
    hazelnut spread 42, **43**
  hummus 40–1
  one-pan cauliflower and Carlin
    pea curry **162**, 163
  oven-cooked chickpeas 132,
    133
chickpea flour
  socca with asparagus and
    creamed cannellini 112
  vegetable fritters 126
children 119–20, 183
chimichurri
  Argentinian chimichurri 93
  wild garlic chimichurri 93, 94,
    95
chips, leftover 71
chocolate
  banana, cardamom and dark
    chocolate bites 116, **117**
  chocolate, chickpea and
    hazelnut spread 42, **43**
  chocolate and rum prune
    puddings **84**, 85
chorizo
  mussels with chorizo and cider
  173
citrus fruit 154
  winter citrus salad 147

cleaning hacks, eco 179
climate change 51, 149
cocoa powder 16, 42, 85
coconut milk/cream/yogurt 14
coffee 137
communal eating 183
composting 71, 106–7
conservation areas 89
containers, food 156, 180
convenience foods 7
cooking, energy saving tips 178
cordial, elderflower 90, 137, 147
courgette 139
  instant pickled 47
cravings 7
crisps, vegetable peeling 70
croutons 64, **65**, 142
cucumber, instant pickled 47
curry
  creamy curried mussels 173
  one-pan cauliflower and Carlin
    pea curry **162**, 163

D
dairy 7
dairy alternatives 81
dal 44, **45**
  tarkas 46
date labels 53–4, 80
date(s) 30, 74
defrosting food 156
dehydration 137
depression 108
desserts 115
  banana, cardamom and dark
    chocolate bites 116, **117**
  chocolate and rum prune
    puddings **84**, 85
  plum and almond upside down
    cake 174, **175**
diabetes, type 2 20, 134
diets
  vegan 8, 17, 68
  vegetarian 8, 68, 97
  weight loss 114, 115
diversity

dietary 26
see also biodiversity
dressings 30, **31**, 70, 104, **105**, 125, 135
    Asian dressing 125
    French vinaigrette 125
drinks
    fizzy 137
    hot 115, 137
    see also water

E
'Eat the Rainbow' mantra 68, 146
eating out 114, 115, 134–5
edamame bean 157
egg 17, 53
    banana, cardamom and dark chocolate bites 116, **117**
    chocolate and rum prune puddings 85
    egg substitutes 17
    plum and almond upside down cake 174
    poached egg with mushroom and lentil ragu 159
    vegan binding recipe 27
elderberry 89
elderflower 90
    cordial 90, 137, 147
endosperm 20, 21
energy-saving tips 178
escalivada (Spanish charred vegetables) 130
ethical considerations 8, 12, 76
ethylene 54

F
Fairtrade 13
farmed fish 168, 171
farming
    environmental impact 76
    intensive 34, 76–7
    local 149, 150
    mega/factory farms 76, 81
    regenerative 34, 77
    subsistence 89

sustainable 34–5, 81
fats 14, 64
fava bean
    roasted beetroot, pot barley and warm fava 'hummus' 22, **23**
fennel 48, 70, 92, 97, 109, 111, 143, 169
fermented foods 15, 48–9
feta 129
    tomato, nectarine, mint and feta 147
fibre 8, 20, 26, 36, 146
fish 8
    fish stock 102
    mackerel with rhubarb salsa 140, **141**
    preserved 169
    seasonal 59
    super-simple fish stew 169
    sustainable 168–9, 171
    'the big five' 168
flatbreads 128
flax milk 81
flaxseed 17, 27, 29, 99, 129
    berry and flaxseed jam **32**, 33
flour 16–17, 20
food choice 115, 119–20
food miles 5, 149
food preferences 7
'food prints' 81, 97
food recycling 106–7
food shopping 12–13, 19, 36, 52–3, 59
food system
    and interconnectivity 7
    and labour shortages 52
    reshaping 12

food waste 51–4, 70–1, 80, 106–7, 142–4
foraging 89
forbidden foods, desire for 7
Forestry Commission 89
freekeh 21
freezer audits 156
freezer containers 156

freezer labels 156
freezing food 54, 80, 154–7, 169
French bean 139
French vinaigrette 125
friands 116, **117**
fridges 54
fritters, vegetable 126, **127**
fruit 54, 146–7
    dried 16, 24, 135
    and food miles 149
    grilled 147
    grow your own 108
    locally grown 149
    loose 180
    orchards 149–50
    purée 154
    seasonal 58–9, 149–50
    stewed 147
    see also specific fruit
fruit juice 146
fungi, soil 34

G
galette, mushroom and tarragon 164–5
gardening 108–9, 111
garlic butter, warm 164–5
geranium, scented (pelargonium) **110**, 111
germ 20, 21
ginger and carrot soup 63
glass 180
global warming 34, 76
grains 19–20, 178
    cracked 21
    polished 21
    rolled 21
granola, homemade 24
gravy 97
greenhouse gases 7, 51, 76, 81, 107
    see also methane
greens 157
    bubble and squeak 100
    bulgur, butter bean and summer greens salad with salsa verde **138**, 139

steam-fried greens **72**, 73, 97
grow your own 108–9, 111, 119, 183
guinea fowl stock 102
gut microbiome (gut bacteria/
    flora) 20, 26, 48, 146

H
habitat loss 51, 76
haricot bean **38**, 39
hazelnut 160
    celeriac and hazelnut soup 63
    chocolate, chickpea and
        hazelnut spread 42, **43**
hazelnut milk 81
heart disease 20, 134
hemp milk 81
herb oils 64
herb and olive seasoning 79
herb stalks 70
herbal teas 90, 137
herbs 155, 159
    dried 16
    and flatbreads 128
    grow your own 108, 111
    herby sauces 92–3, 94, **95**
hoverfly 111
hummus 40–1, **40**
    butter bean and beetroot 41
    cannellini and pesto 41
    simple chickpea 41
    smoky black bean and
        peanut 41
    warm fava 'hummus' 22, **23**
hunger, global 51
'hungry gap, the' 89
hunter-gatherers 68, 89, 119

I
ice cream, banana 154
induction hobs 178

J
jam, berry and flaxseed **32**, 33
Japanese Bokashi bins 107
Jerusalem artichoke soup 60, **61**
junk food 20, 115, 120

K
kale 67, 125
    bubble and squeak 100
    smoked quinoa, kale and apple
        salad 30, **31**
kettles 178
kimchi 15
kitchens, green 177–83
kohlrabi 30, 48, 73–4

L
lactic acid 49
ladybirds 111
lamb 76
    mushroom and lentil ragu 158
    party food: slow-roasted
        pulled shoulder of lamb
        132, **133**
larders 7–8, 54
lectin 37
leek 71, 173
    leek and pumpkin speltotto
        with crumbled blue cheese
        82, **83**
leftovers 70–1, 80, 100, 156
legumes 36
    see also specific legumes
lemon 154
    lemon sauce 160, **161**
lentil(s) (green)
    mushroom and lentil ragu
        158–9, **159**
    warm lentil salad with roasted
        radish, whipped cheese and
        wild garlic chimichurri 94, **95**
lentil(s) (red), dal 44, **45**
lettuce 124–5
lime 154
livestock 76, 77–8, 81, 106
loaf, simple seeded spelt 25
local food producers 12, 13, 149,
    150, 183
lunch boxes 134–5

M
mackerel with rhubarb salsa 140, **141**

maize 26
marigold 111
Marine Conservation Society
    (MCS) 168
Marine Stewardship Council
    (MSC) 168
markets 12
meal plans 53
meat 7, 8
    'affordable' 76
    better 77
    eating less 76
    monthly roast 97
    pasture-fed 77
    red 76
    seasonal 59
    see also beef; lamb
mental health 108
methane 76, 106
milk 54, 80–1
    see also plant-based milk
milk bottles 180
minestrone **66**, 67
moules marinières 172
muhammara (Syrian pepper and
    walnut dip) 131
multibuys 53
mushroom 79
    dried 14
    mushroom and lentil ragu
        158–9, **159**
    mushroom and tarragon
        galette 164–5
mussels 171–3
    creamy curried mussels 173
    moules marinières 172
    mussels with chorizo and
        cider 173
mustard 15
mycelia 34

N
nasturtium **110**, 111
National Nature Reserves (NNRs)
    89
National Trust 89, 136

nature 108
nectarine
   nectarine, raspberry, thyme
      and toasted almonds 147
   tomato, nectarine, mint and
      feta 147
nettle 90
nitrogen fixation 36
noodles, Asian chicken noodle
   soup 103
nut butters 14
nut milks 81
nutritional yeast 14, 92
nuts 19, 24, 27, 74, 92, 135
   see also hazelnut; walnut

O
oat groats 21
oat milks 81
oat(s) (rolled) 24, 129
obesity 7, 20, 114
oils 14
olive 15
   herb and olive seasoning 79
onion, pink onion pickle 47
orchards 149–50
organic produce 13, 17, 34–5, 81
oven cleaners 179
ovens 178
overweight 134

P
packaging 5, 124, 134, 179, 180
packed lunches 134–5
pancakes, buckwheat 29
panzanella salad 143
Parmesan 14, 112, 160
   bean burgers 129
   cabbage and Parmesan slaw 74
   Jerusalem artichoke soup 60
   minestrone 67
   pesto 92
   rind 67, 80, 103, 159
parsnip 74
   spiced parsnip soup 63
   vegetable peeling crisps 70

party food: slow-roasted pulled
   shoulder of lamb 132, **133**
pasta 53
   Italian-style brodo 103
   minestrone 67
pastry
   mushroom and tarragon
      galette 164–5
   puff pastry 157
pea shoots 104, 109
peanut, smoky black bean and
   peanut hummus 41
pear 74
   pears with sheep's cheese and
      honey 147
pearl barley 79
pea(s) 157
pepper 129, 159, 163
   muhammara 131
   smoky peppers and aubergines
      130–1
pesto 92
   cannellini and pesto
      hummus 41
pests 111
phytochemicals 146
pickles
   instant pickled cucumber/
      courgette 47
   pink onion pickle 47
   quick pickles 47
   spiced carrot or cauliflower
      pickle 47
pie, cottage garden 159
plant foods 183
plant-based milk 81, 180
plastic 81, 136, 180
plum 150
   plum and almond upside-down
      cake 174, **175**
pollinators 111
pomegranate molasses 15
population growth, global 51, 76
portion size 114
pot barley 21
   roasted beetroot, pot barley

and warm fava 'hummus'
   22, **23**
potato 54
   bubble and squeak 100
   celebration spring salad 104
   and food waste 70–1
   minestrone 67
   super-simple fish stew 169
   vegetable peeling crisps 70
poultry stock 102–3
prebiotics 48
pressure cookers 37, 178
probiotics 48
processed foods 20
   see also ultra-processed foods
protein
   animal sources 8, 76, 77
   vegetarian/vegan 8, 27, 76
prune, chocolate and rum prune
   puddings **84**, 85
pseudocereals 27
puff pastry 157
pulse flour 17
pulses 19, 36, 53, 135, 155, 178
   boiling 37
   canned/jars 36
   cooking from scratch 37
   dried 36
   soaking 37
   'water print' 76
pumpkin
   leek and pumpkin speltotto
      with crumbled blue cheese
      82, **83**
   mushroom and lentil ragu
      158–9
pumpkin seed 24
purées
   fruit 154
   vegetable 97, 155

Q
quinoa 24, 27
   smoked quinoa, kale and apple
      salad 30, **31**

R

radish 71, 92, 104
  warm lentil salad with roasted radish, whipped cheese and wild garlic chimichurri 94, **95**
ragu, mushroom and lentil 158–9, **159**
rainbow slaw 74, **75**
raspberry, thyme, toasted almonds and nectarine 147
recycling 106–7, 180, 183
red cabbage
  rainbow slaw 74, **75**
  simple ruby sauerkraut 48
red kidney bean(s)
  bean burgers 129
  boiling 37
refill stores 12, 180
rhubarb salsa with mackerel 140, **141**
rice 21, 26
'ricotta', homemade 80
roast dinners **96**, 97–100
  party food: slow-roasted pulled shoulder of lamb 132, **133**
  roast chicken **96**, 97, 98
  veggie 97
'root-to-fruit' eating 70–1, 92
rum and chocolate prune puddings **84**, 85
ruminants 76–7
runner bean 139
rye berries 21
rye flakes 24

S

salad leaves 108–9, 124–5
salads 119, 135
  bulgur, butter bean and summer greens salad with salsa verde **138**, 139
  celebration spring salad 104, **105**
  grow your own 108–9
  panzanella salad 143

smoked quinoa, kale and apple salad 30, **31**
  warm lentil salad with roasted radish, whipped cheese and wild garlic chimichurri 94, **95**
  winter citrus salad 147
salsa, rhubarb 140, **141**
salsa verde **138**, 139
salt 14
sardines 140
sauces
  fermented 15
  herby 92–3
  lemon 160, **161**
sauerkraut 15, 48
  simple ruby 48
seafood 171
seasons 8
  eating by the 58–9
  see also autumn; spring; summer; winter
seaweed 15, 89
seeds 19, 27, 135
  and flatbreads 128
  oily 19, 27, 92
  rainbow slaw 74
  savoury 28
  simple seeded spelt loaf 25
  simple toasted 28
  sprinkles 28
  tamari 28
  warm spiced 28
  see also specific seeds
shallot 60
sheep's cheese, pears with sheep's cheese and honey 147
shopping, food 12–13, 19, 36, 52–3, 59
Sites of Special Scientific Interest (SSSIs) 89
slaw
  cabbage and Parmesan 74
  rainbow 74, **75**
sloe 89
slow cookers 178
smoking, fish 169

smoothies 146
snacks, healthy 120, 147
socca with asparagus and creamed cannellini 112, **113**
soil quality 34–5
soup 70, 71
  Asian chicken noodle 103
  creamed vegetable 62–3, **63**
  Jerusalem artichoke 60, **61**
  minestrone **66**, 67
  nettle 90
  toppings for 64, **65**
sour powders, dry 15
soya milk 81
spelt 21, 24
  leek and pumpkin speltotto with crumbled blue cheese 82, **83**
  simple seeded spelt loaf 25
spices 16, 128
spinach 29, 157
spread, chocolate, chickpea and hazelnut 42, **43**
spring 87–121
spring onion 71
squash 158–9
  roast squash and black bean tacos 166, **167**
  squash and rosemary soup 63
sterilisation 49
stew 70
  'eke out the meat', beef **78**, 79
  super-simple fish 169
stock 70, 102–3, 155
store cupboard ingredients 14–17
strawberries and elderflower cordial 147
stroke 20, 134
stuffing balls 97, 99
sugar 137
sugar alternatives 16
summer 123–51
summer pudding 144, **145**
sunflower seed 24
sustainability 13, 34–5, 81, 168, 171
swede 159

sweeteners 16
Swiss chard 67

T

tacos, roast squash and black bean 166, **167**
tahini 14, 40, 64, 131
takeaways 114
tamarind 15
tarkas 46
tarragon 16, 64, 98, 164–5
tea 137
    herbal 90, 137
    nettle 90
tomato 15, 58
    baked beans 39
    mushroom and lentil ragu 158–9
    nectarine, mint and feta 147
    one-pan cauliflower and Carlin pea curry 163
    panzanella salad 143
    roasted celeriac with tomato and lemon sauce 160, **161**
    sun-dried 15
    zaalouk 131
tomato purée 15
tortillas
    frozen 157
    roast squash and black bean tacos 166
turkey stock 102
turnip tops 71

U

ultra-processed foods 7, 20, 115, 134
umami 14, 15, 79, 97, 159, 169
United Nations Educational, Scientific and Cultural Organization (UNESCO) 76
'use-by' dates 53, 80

V

vegan diet 8, 17, 68
vegetables 135

Asian chicken noodle soup 103
creamed vegetable soup 62–3, **63**
    bubble and squeak 97, 100, **101**
    eating more 68
    'eke out the meat', beef stew 79
    escalivada (Spanish charred vegetables) 130
    grow your own 108–9, 111
    leftover 97
    loose 180
    minestrone 67
    peelings 70–1
    purées 97, 155
    roast 97
    roasted celeriac with tomato and lemon sauce 160, **161**
    seasonal 58–9
    shopping for 13
    tops 71
    vegetable fritters 126, **127**
    vegetable purée 155
    vegetable stock 102
    wonky 51
    see also specific vegetables
vegetarian diet 8, 68, 97
vinaigrette, French 125
vinegar 15, 47
    white (spirit vinegar) 179

W

walnut 30, 129, 164–5
    muhammara 131
waste 51–4, 70–1, 80, 106–7, 142–4
Waste and Resources Action Programme, The (WRAP) 52, 80
water
    bottled 136
    scarcity 76
    tap 137
    'water print' 76
weight loss diets 114, 115
wheat 24, 26
wheat berries 21
whole foods 20, 48, 115, 183
whole grains 19, 20–1, 135

wholemeal flour 17
wild garlic (ransoms) 90
    chimichurri 93, 94, **95**
wildlife 7
winter 57–85
Woodland Trust 89
Worcestershire sauce 15
World Wildlife Fund (WWF) 81
worm tea 106–7
wormeries 106–7

Y

Yorkshire pudding 97

Z

zaalouk (Moroccan aubergine and tomato) 131
zero waste stores 52, 179, 180, 184

Acknowledgments

HUGE THANKS:

To Peter Taylor at HarperCollins, and to The National Trust, for giving me the opportunity to write a book that I feel so passionately about.

To Kathy Steer for such patient and thorough copy-editing and to Sarah Pyke for her brilliant design. To Katie Hewett for helping to make it all fit together. To Verity Rimmer, Chloe McIntosh and Felicity Roos at the National Trust for their corrections and suggestions.

To my great mate Sally Macgill for her very frank comments and suggestions about the information pages, I so appreciate both your genuine interest and your time.

To Kirstie Young for wonderful photography, and to the fabulous Anna Shepherd for helping to cook and style the shoot. We made a great team: beautiful pictures and so much fun along the way. To all the local potters, gardeners and independent suppliers who gave us such stunning props and food to play with.

To all the farmers and gardeners of the National Trust and the wider community who work with nature to produce our food and nurture our environment. And equally to all the shops and suppliers who champion them and sell their wares – you are what this book is all about.

Lastly to my rocks: Imi and Peter, and to all the neighbours and friends who have eaten their way through the recipes, often on repeat, until I cracked the dish; I love you all.

Photo credits

All photographs by Kirstie Young, except:

Shutterstock: 12, 15, 16, 26, 8, 36, 50, 81, 109, 120, 142, 150, 151, 154, 155, 157, 170, 176–7, 180.

National Trust Images: 35 (NTI/John Miller), 77 (NTI/Nick Upton), 88 (NTI/Hilary Daniel), 91 (NTI/Robert Morris), 118 (NTI/Arnhel de Serra), 148 (NTI/James Dobson), 159 (NTI/William Shaw).

Back cover photographs: Kirstie Young